How To Survive An Attack

by
Roberts Liardon

Embassy Publishing
Laguna Hills, CA 92654

Unless otherwise indicated, all Scripture quotations are taken from the *King James Version* of the Bible.

Some Scripture quotations are taken from the *Amplified Bible, New Testament*. Copyright © 1954, 1958 by The Lockman Foundation, La Habra, California.

3rd Printing

How To Survive An Attack
ISBN 1-879993-00-7

Copyright © 1991 by Embassy Publishing Co.
P.O. Box 3500
Laguna Hills, CA 92654-0710

Published by Embassy Publishing Co.
P.O. Box 3500
Laguna Hills, California 92654

Contents

 **Roberts Liardon** was born in Tulsa, Oklahoma. He was born again, baptized in the Holy Spirit, and called to the ministry at the age of eight, after being caught up to Heaven by the Lord Jesus.

Roberts was powerfully commissioned by the Lord to study the lives of God's great "generals" — men and women of faith who were mightily used by God in the past — in order to learn why they succeeded and why they failed.

At age fourteen, Roberts began preaching and teaching in various churches — denominational, non-denominational alike — Bible colleges and universities. He has traveled extensively in the United States and Canada, and his missions outreaches have taken him to Africa, Europe, and Asia. Many of his books have been translated into foreign languages.

Roberts preaches and ministers under a powerful anointing of the Holy Spirit. In his sermons, Roberts calls people of all ages to salvation, holiness and life in the Holy Spirit.

Through Roberts' ministry around the world, many people have accepted God's call to yield themselves as vessels for the work of the Kingdom.

Chapter 1

Knowing Your Enemy

It was three o'clock in the morning. My room was dark and wonderfully quiet and I was doing what most people should be doing at that particular hour — *sleeping!*

I had just returned from an exhausting schedule of ministry. The meetings had been good and lives were changed. I was happy and at peace. Everything was calm and in order and I was totally relaxed, enjoying my rest.

But things were about to change.

All of a sudden, the shrill ringing of my telephone pierced the night and abruptly ended my moment of comfort. I fumbled the telephone receiver to my ear and from the other end a frantic voice whined, "Roberts! Roberts! Help me... help me."

As I listened to the circumstances of my distraught friend, I interrupted and said, "You are not seeing clearly. This is not a problem — it's the devil."

"The devil?" He was shocked.

"That's right. It's the devil. You are under attack and don't even know it."

As I continued to talk with him into the wee hours of the morning, I began to realize that many Christians do not know the tactics of their enemy. They may be good, faithful people, filled with the love and zeal of God, and still be totally ignorant when it comes to the schemes of the devil.

As believers, we should not be afraid to discuss the devil. Jesus mentioned and taught about him very often in the New Testament. Jesus did not *exalt* the devil by discussing him. He *exposed* him by teaching the disciples of his devices.

Understand this principle: Exposing the devil is not our priority; *knowing God is*. But anything that hinders our relationship with God, or attempts to abort His plan in the earth, must be dealt with and properly understood.

Jesus came and taught the Truth about God, exposing the lies the enemy had perpetrated against Him. And on the other hand, He dealt openly with the devil and his demons and taught the people their authority over him.

The Apostle Paul writes in 2 Corinthians 2:11:

> **Lest Satan should get an advantage of us: for we are not ignorant of his devices.**

We have a mandate, a commission from God to know our enemy. If we as believers do not understand or comprehend his tactics, then the Bible says he will get an advantage over us. If we do not know the way our enemy operates, then he will have the ability to deceive us and cause us to waste our lives.

We who are born again have been purchased and bought by the Blood of Jesus. As believers, it is true we enter into the benefits of the finished works of Christ. But nowhere does Scripture teach that the new birth automatically eliminates demonic *influence* or demonic *attack*. Jesus Himself personally dealt with the enemy in the wilderness (Luke 4) and throughout His public ministry as well. The disciples, even as they were personally with Jesus Himself, had to also stand against the schemes of the devil in their own lives. Peter attempted to persuade Jesus not to go to the Cross in Matthew 16:20-22. And although he vowed undying loyalty, Jesus told him he would deny Him three times; which he did (Matthew 26:33-34,74). Demonic power influenced one of the disciples to betray Him (Matthew 26:21-25). When James and John did not like the actions of the Samaritans, Jesus rebuked them and told them, *"ye know not what manner of spirit ye are of"* (Luke 9:54-56). Demonic influence and attack will attempt to come and persuade, no matter what level of maturity we walk in.

The first part of Hosea 4:6 states,

> *My people are destroyed for lack of know-*
> *ledge...*

Lack of knowledge in the area of demonic influence has caused many believers to fall and fail. Many open the trap doors of calamity, destruction and even death by not knowing the intention of their enemy.

Part of the last commission Jesus gave us before He left the earth was:

> *...In my name shall they cast out devils...*
>
> *Mark 16:17*

We cannot "cast out" something we do not know nor understand.

Ignorance makes us immobile. It causes us to remain passive in an area, because we do not understand it. Ignorance gives ground and entrance to the schemes of the devil. *Ignorance works for the enemy because it gives him freedom to pursue and conquer without being noticed.*

When we do not properly discern the schemes of the enemy, it will negatively affect our churches, our nation and every other sphere of our lives. **We must preach and know the whole Gospel; not just a part of it.** When we refuse to recognize our enemy, we will become a prey to him. When we shrink away from Truth and refuse to examine it or learn from it, then we remain unprepared for the attacks of a raging enemy.

The Bible is not ashamed to discuss and expose the devil. From Genesis to Revelation, the entire plan and purpose of our enemy unfolds. It is our responsibility to train and mature ourselves through the Word, through prayer, the leading of the Holy Spirit, and the godly authority that God has positioned over us.

Because some believers fail to take the responsibility of maturing themselves, the plan of God is thwarted in their lives. As a result, some are trying to live in the midst of an attack and cannot see nor understand **why they act the way they do** or **think the way they may think.** They think instead it is just their personality or their circumstances.

I am not saying that every negative situation we face is a demon, because I don't believe it is. Many times we find ourselves in trouble because of undisciplined flesh and desires. We are not dealing with that side in this book. Understand that trouble comes several ways, two being: **uncontrolled flesh** and **demonic influence.** The purpose of this book, however, is to enlighten our walk as believers, to the attacks of the enemy.

The Word of God was written for our instruction, to teach and train us. Written on the pages of the Bible are truths of life, health and peace. If we fall, through those truths we can stand again. Through embracing those truths, we are healed if sickness comes. As we mature our inner man through prayer and the Word, we don't have to fall prey to deception. We can effectively stand, prevail and conquer when an attack comes. Embrace the Word of God as your safeguard. Jesus said it in John 10:10; *believe it.* Through Him, we can have life, and *Life* more abundantly!

Chapter 2

How To Recognize An Attack

In the natural realm of life, we have several different branches of the military that train and equip themselves to do battle. These men and women undergo extensive drills to learn the strategy of their enemy. Not only do they train themselves in expertise with their weaponry; they also are alerted to learn the conditions for an attack and the situations that are conducive to one.

The natural military is loyal and committed to protect what is theirs by boundary. They know the importance of unity in winning a battle. They are drilled in diligence and skill for the sake of their nation and loved ones.

The diligence they underwent in training pays off when a surprise attack comes. The months they spent jumping up at the crack of dawn and the repeated examination of their weapons causes them to be able to respond without much thought. The constant drill places a *law* inside of them; *not a formula*. The weeks of crawling through a field on their chest with live bullets flying overhead has caused them to face obstacles without fear. They are trained and equipped.

The natural military develops a bond with their weapons. They would not think of approaching enemy territory without them. Picture it. A soldier unarmed would be a joke! They know where a land mine is probable; they can detect an approaching enemy; they know when to take cover and when to attack. The natural military is secure because of their preparation and insight.

It is easy in the natural to recognize an attack. You can hear the bombs explode, the torpedoes drop and the machine guns fire.

An attack in the spirit can alert us much in the same way. The problem is, we have not taken the time to train ourselves, so we turn a "deaf ear" to the sound of the enemy. Then we "wake up" and wonder why we are in the condition we're in!

The sad thing is, when the battle is over, it is easy to say, "That was the devil." As believers, we should know **before** the battle ever starts that it is him, the devil.

Just as soldiers in the natural train for conflict, we must train for spiritual conflict.

Godly Confrontation

We don't just wake up one day and our home has fallen apart. We don't just look around and our children have run away from home. We don't just get up some morning and find we are in total poverty. It starts someplace. The first time you felt an impression that something was not right, what did you do? **Did you ignore it or confront it?**

When we ignore a bad situation, it will continue to worsen. The devil won't go away if you leave him an open door. Uncontrolled desires will not disappear. Ignoring destructive situations will cause the downfall of your family, your health or your circumstances.

Let us build within us the ability of godly confrontation. Godly confrontation results from a mature inner man, seasoned by the Word of God. Sometimes when we hear the word "confront," we think of loud aggression. I'm not talking about brash, rude confronting. I'm speaking of the confrontation that "destroys the yoke of bondage."

Sometimes confronting comes by a soft answer. Sometimes the evil plans are confronted by an action — a counteraction by good. And yes, sometimes confrontation is loud. There are times when a person has been led so far by the enemy, he must be "jerked" back into reality. But always remember whatever way the Holy Spirit leads you to confront, **godly results are produced.** A soft answer, a counteraction or a loud confrontation are *all direct* and *productive* when you are led by God. They are *all* works of boldness. Jesus was the meekest man on earth; but He was not weak. He never failed to confront the works of the devil. He spoke the truth; but His methods of presentation were according to each circumstance.

Test The Source

Don't believe the lie: "Well, some things happen for the glory of God." God does not redeem us from something and then test us with it. He doesn't put sickness, disease, death or poverty on us to teach humility. He will not cause you to go through something He paid for at the Cross. So many talk doubt and unbelief, giving glory to the enemy while thinking they are being humble for God.

The enemy will come and whisper, "You are an unworthy soul." You might say, "That's right." Then he'll say, "God is going to teach you something through sickness and disease." Again you respond, "That's right." The next thing you know, we're burying you.

We must know the character of God to recognize an attack. If we really know Who God is and how He operates, then we will be able to detect and destroy the devices of the enemy.

The Bible says in John 10:10:

The thief cometh not, but for to steal and to kill, and to destroy: I am come that they might have life, and that they might have it more abundantly.

If we have lessons to learn, then learn them through prayer, the Word and godly leadership. Why suffer under the hand of the enemy, blame God, and then if you live through it, say you've "learned something?"

Temptation and Wiles

The devil plans his attack. He has a strategy in every situation. The first step in recognizing an attack is understanding the devil will work his strategy in one of two ways: by *wiles* or *temptations*.

Temptations are obvious. They are outright, blatant words, exposures or situations. The Bible says in James 1:14 that we can only fall into temptation through our own lusts that have gone undealt with. Understand that *God* does *not* tempt you (verse 13). The enemy will use a temptation against you in an area that has caused you trouble in the past. Temptation comes as a way the enemy plans to abort you from the will of God. It is an attack designed for you to sin, to harden your heart against the Spirit of the Lord.

Temptations can cause heaviness and depression. Sometimes they come in manifold numbers. But those that trust in the Lord at these times are safe and secure. Second Peter 2:9 says, *"The Lord knoweth how to deliver the godly out of temptations..."*

The Bible says that every man is tempted. Hebrews 4:15 says Jesus Himself, *"was in all points tempted like as we are, yet without sin."* His identification with us and His death on the Cross paid for our freedom from the clutches of temptation.

12

The second strategy of the devil is through the means of a *wile*. *A wile is a scheme that is hidden to deceive. It is not obvious like a temptation.* A wile intends to lure you as if by a magic spell. It craftily covers itself to lead you into deception.

Although the Bible only uses the word "wiles" once in the New Testament, Scripture repeatedly warns us of deceptions.

The Bible is clear when Scripture speaks of deception.

Those who have embraced a wile are deceived when:

They are a hearer of the Word and not a doer (James 1:22).

They think they have no sin (I John 1:8).

They think they are something when they are nothing (Galatians 6:3).

They think they are wise with the wisdom of the world (I Corinthians 3:18).

They have an unbridled tongue yet they never miss church (James 1:26).

They think they can sow and not reap what they've sown (Galatians 6:7).

They think the unrighteous can inherit the Kingdom of God (I Corinthians 6:9).

They think contact and communion with sin will not have an effect on them (I Corinthians 15:33).

They think they can lie, have no remorse for sin and not depart from the faith (I Timothy 4:1-3).

Truth is the only antidote for deception. We can be alerted to every scheme if we will listen to our spirits. You may not understand it completely, but back away until you do. Judge everything by the Truth of the Scripture and the character of God. Those two safeguards will ground an enemy missile every time.

Demonic Rank

Another way to recognize an attack is to discern the level of your enemy. Just as we mentioned before, the devil has rank, order and governments in his kingdom. It is important that we know who they are.

In Ephesians 6:12, the Apostle Paul categorized the ranks of evil spirits. He said:

> *For we wrestle not against flesh and blood, but against principalities, against powers, against the rulers of the darkness of this world, against spiritual wickedness in high places.*

Every evil spirit has their assigned position. To recognize the level of attack, we must see their sphere of influence.

Principalities are the force and dominion that deals with nations and governments. That is their regime. The order of the government in a nation and the economy of the world can be influenced by these principalities.

Powers have authority and power to take action in any sphere that is open to them. Wherever entrance is given that will affect a multitude, the work of an evil power will be searching for an opening.

World rulers are evil spirits that govern the darkness and blindness of the world, keeping them from seeing the wickedness and deception they are in.

Wicked spirits operate from heavenly places. Their target is the church, and their method is wiles and deceptions. Fiery darts, onslaughts, doctrines of devils and every false work are feats they are capable of planning.

There are also demons that are of a low degree. To be

honest with you, these spirits are dumb. They scream, holler, harass, aggravate and mean absolutely nothing. They have a little bit of power, but they can only bother us if we fear them.

The high ranking spirits are very smart, and they watch. They watch what you say, they watch where you look and they watch where you go. Then, just as our natural military do, they go back with their information and plan a strategy against you. Their purpose is to destroy you and the Church.

That is one reason why great ministries have fallen. A high level strategy attack was implemented against them and it was not recognized until it was too late. We will never recognize an attack of the enemy unless we learn his methods.

Symptoms of an Attack

The enemy will attack in your mind, your body and your spirit. I will discuss these areas in the chapters to come. But before we discuss those areas in detail, there are some basic signals we need to be alerted to.

Number one, when a person is under attack, they lose their spiritual hunger for God.

Just as physical appetite leaves a person who is sick in their body, it is also the first thing to hit and leave a person under spiritual attack. They are not hungry for the things of God. They don't want to go to church, they don't want to pray, they don't want to read their Bible and to be blunt, they don't really care about God at that moment. They like Him; but He's more like Number 4 instead of Number 1 in their lives.

Since our spiritual hunger is the first thing the enemy will attack in us, we must protect it at all costs. Matthew 5:6 says:

Blessed are they which do hunger and thirst after righteousness: for they shall be filled.

If we do not hunger and thirst for the things of God and His character, there will be no infilling. An empty vessel will be filled with something — good or evil. Choose to protect that which is God and build upon it with the Word.

Even when you might not feel like reading the Bible, pick it up and read it anyway! The Bible is alive even when you feel dead. The written Word of God is one of your weapons of warfare. Learn to pull it out and feed yourself to sustain the life inside of you. The natural military does not always feel like pulling out their rifles, taking them apart, cleaning them and putting them back together. But they know and understand that weapon will save their life in combat. The same is true for the written Word of God. You may not always feel like taking it out, reading it, letting it adjust and cleanse you; but it will be your shield and buckler in spiritual combat.

When your desire for God leaves, it gives entrance to the enemy.

Have you ever seen a person who was really on fire for God get "hit" by the enemy and fade away? How could someone with so much zeal now be so backslidden?

Did you ever see someone expressive and free in praise and worship now be suddenly still and cold?

The enemy has won over their hunger and desire for God and now they have no motivation. Spiritual hunger is motivation to go on with God, just as physical hunger motivates you to eat. Spiritual hunger is an acquired taste. It sustains life.

People who are alcoholics have acquired the taste. There is no way a person can normally like alcohol. They trick themselves to continue in drinking it until they acquire the taste and desire for it. They have become addicted and cannot live without it.

Spiritual hunger is an acquired desire and taste as well.

How do you become spiritually hungry? How do you stay spiritually hungry? It's simple. It's not always easy, but it's simple. You walk your bedroom floor and make yourself get hungry for God. You say out of your mouth, "I want more of You, God." Even when your mind says, "No you don't," you say, "Yes I do. Shut up."

You have to learn to talk to yourself and tell yourself how to think. That is how you take control of your mind and teach it to flow with the Word of God.

God cannot use someone who is divided within themselves. If your mind is thinking of cooking the evening meal, and your flesh is doing something else — and the whole time you are praying, it is a divided prayer. **A fervent prayer that produces results is one whose mind agrees, his flesh is subdued and the spirit leads them all.** You have got to be together, spirit, mind and body. That kind of prayer will see results. That is the prayer of a righteous man.

When you are under the attack of the devil, you must make yourself hungry for the things of God. Think about the time you were sick and you did not want to eat. What was the first thing someone who cared about you did? They put food in front of you and said, "Eat."

You probably said, "I don't want to eat this. I'm not hungry." They said, "I don't care. Eat it." Why? Because they know the nutrients in that food will strengthen your body and help it to overcome weakness. It will give you a force to overcome physical sickness.

It is the same in the realm of the Spirit. When you are under the fire of the devil, that is not the time to quit going

17

to church. That is not the time to quit reading the Word of God and confessing and praying. That is not the time to stop your labor for God. Instead, *that is the time to turn it up!*

Understand that the goal of the enemy is to rid you of spiritual desire for God. If you give in to it, you'll go under. It is only your Word level, your prayer level and people of like faith that cause you to go over. **You've got to stay around people that give you life when you are in a war.** Don't hang around "dead beats." Do you know what I mean by that? Don't hang around lifeless, negative, carnal people. **Above all, don't isolate yourself.** Find someone that's "perking." Find someone with spunk and zeal for God. Their influence will help you and strengthen you in a time of trouble. The Bible says a good friend will sharpen you (Proverbs 27:17).

The second thing that happens to a person under attack is a loss of strength. Even though they are smiling and saying the same things, they have lost that force about them. They don't have what I call the "bam!" in them. They have lost their spiritual punch and accuracy. There is no life, joy or jump in them.

In Ephesians chapter 6, verse 10, Paul says:

Finally, my brethren, be strong in the Lord, and in the power of his might.

True joy, strength and life comes from the inward man. The only way a believer can effectively fight an attack is by gaining their strength from the Lord. **You cannot win outside of the spirit.** Allow your confession in the Word of God to give you strength: *"Let the weak say, I AM STRONG."*

We must be careful not to rely on natural ability when we are in a spiritual war. When we are more comfortable with soulish and natural strengths than we are spiritual strengths, we end up helping the enemy. That is why sometimes, in a church-wide battle, there are disastrous splits and calamity, because believers go from spiritual combat into natural combat. They fall prey to mental ability. Natural combat uses its strength in cutting and slanderous words. Gossip and fear are its weapons.

We must learn to recognize the attack of the enemy in the area of spiritual strength. We must learn to stand and fight with the Word of God and in the realm of the Spirit. If leadership can remain in the Spirit and gain their strength from the Lord, the battle will not be as disastrous.

When the natural body is sick, every part of the body is focused on the attack inside of it. To win in the Spirit, the focus must be the same. When you are under attack, all of your energy must come from the strength you have built in the Lord to overcome it. You must keep your strength up and not grow weak.

The third way to recognize an attack is that you don't feel like yourself.

When the natural body is sick, you feel terrible. We have a tendency to be short with people. We usually act gripey and bossy even to those we love the most. We don't feel like ourselves, we feel strange and we act strange. When the body is sick, our natural tendency is to lay on the sofa, watch television; or go to bed and sleep the day away.

Learn to recognize a spiritual attack in the same way. When you are being fought by the enemy, whether it is totally demonic or maneuvered through a human being, you begin to feel things that are not true. One of those feelings is paranoia. Do you know what I mean by that? You begin to feel like you are being judged, criticized and that everyone is looking at you and telling you how awfully wrong you are. You feel like you can never please anyone because your life is such a spectacle. If you give in to those feelings, you'll quit and go backwards. That is called an attack of the devil.

19

When these feelings come to you, learn how to reject them. You must learn to stand, resist and fight back! Do not give into them, retreat and say, "Well, I must just be this way. I'll never do anything for God because I am no good." If you say that, the enemy has won.

I used to go through wars, and it would take me a while to figure out what I was in. I just thought, "Lord, I'm tired." I wanted to retreat, sit at home and watch television. The saddest thing you can do when you are in a spiritual war is to watch television. Television is not wrong, but at that particular time in your life all it will do is feed your soul and take over your weak spirit. The next worse thing you can do is go to bed and pretend the world doesn't exist. Your soul will sometimes "tilt" in spiritual warfare, so it will want to sleep and not deal with the reality around it. But the truth is, when you wake up, the battle is still there and has possibly gained strength because you refused to fight.

I had to learn that a war is made up of many battles both great and small.

It was hard to pray during those times. As a matter of fact, I would have rather washed dishes than pray! I would say, "God, I don't want to deal with this. Just let me sit and do nothing. Please."

Spiritual warfare drains your physical body. All you want is to sit and do nothing. You don't want to talk; you don't want to eat. You don't want to say, "hi," or even pet a dog. You act like someone has physically beat you up, because that's what is happening in the spirit realm.

When people are in the spirit, they are outgoing. When people are flowing with God, secure in God, they have a joy that just won't end. **Love and joy comes as a way of life when you live in the Spirit.** These people are strong, energetic and aggressive. They focus on their purpose in the Spirit.

I had to learn that when I was in a war, I could not go to a place where there was no battle going on. That was retreat. There are no retreats in the Kingdom of God. There are only charges! When you build your strength in God, you'll have that "charge" no matter what is happening around you.

When you are under fire, you bring out the biggest spiritual gun you have and blow that attack out of its arena. Many times when I am preaching, I can feel myself "hit" the war zone. Sometimes, I just stand up behind the pulpit and never say a word, and I've already entered into it!

Don't ever be intimidated in a spiritual war. Intimidation is a major weapon of the enemy. Intimidation puts you in a box and you can't come out and be yourself. The devil will try to make you feel insecure because anointed preaching exposes him for what he is. The enemy hates anointing. He hates those that know how to walk in it and administer it. The anointing breaks his yoke, his bondage and his chains. It destroys the lies he has caused people to believe. When those bondages are broken, the people are set free and made strong. They don't take any more garbage off the devil and he hates that.

One of the best tactics the enemy can use on a minister is to make him feel rejected, intimidated and insecure. Why? Because it hinders him from speaking the Truth that sets men free. God wants you to be yourself, seasoned with His Word.

You are the victor; so be it. You are more than a conqueror; so conquer. Don't stand there and say, "Well, no one likes me." Say, **"Devil, I break your power!"**

The Bible calls us an "army" and that's not a nice little illustration. The Bible tells us that because we are an army, we must learn the strategies of the enemy and conquer them. Learn to recognize when an attack comes. Stand up to it and win in the strength of the Lord.

Chapter 3

How to Go Through an Attack

We have now established that we have an enemy. We have also learned the first warnings that come with a spiritual attack.

You might have said, "That described me." Once we determine we are in an attack, we need to know how to win in it.

Understand that spiritual attacks will not go away by themselves. You cannot ignore the situation or pretend it does not exist. You cannot involve yourself in some other outlet and hope it will leave you alone if you don't think about it. We must learn how to not only stand against it, but *go through it* in total victory.

Before we can effectively win in an attack, there are some basic things we must realize.

Not The Person...

In Ephesians chapter 6, beginning in verse twelve, Paul tells us:

For we wrestle not against flesh and blood, but against principalities, against powers, against the rulers of the darkness of this world, against spiritual wickedness in high places.

First of all, **you must realize in your heart that you are**

not fighting a person. If you fall into the scheme that you are fighting a *natural* person or problem during a spiritual attack, you will revert to natural means. You will not win if you choose the road of gossip, slander or revenge. **You cannot have soulish discussion to ease spiritual pressure.**

Spiritual warfare means a *spiritual influence* over someone or something. He might come through the same type of attitude through another person; but it will hardly ever be through the same person he previously used. That can only happen if one is still ignorant or open in this area of their life. We will discuss this area in a later chapter, but we must receive the basics of this principle first.

If the devil cannot win over you through a person, he will wait awhile and try for one that is closer to you. He did the same with Jesus.

The enemy attacked the ministry of Jesus through the multitudes and the religious leaders of the day. When He remained unmoved, the devil tried for the disciples. He tried through Peter and several others; but he succeeded in conquering Judas. Even though the attack came through one closest to Him, Jesus knew the source and remained unhindered. He knew His mission, and He kept His eyes on the goal of it. Even on the Cross, He said:

> *Father, forgive them; for they know not what they do.* Luke 23:34

How could He say that? He was showing us a basic principle in surviving an attack. **Jesus was not interrupted by betrayal.** Forgiveness destroys the schemes of the devil. Forgiveness is a force that proves you know your God *and* your enemy. That is why Paul **first** says in 2 Corinthians 2:

> *To whom ye forgive any thing, I forgive also: for if I forgave any thing, to whom I forgave it, for your sakes forgave I it in the person of Christ;*

Lest Satan should get an advantage of us: for we are not ignorant of his devices.

Verses 10,11

Forgiveness puts your focus and trust in the right direction. It will give entrance to the power, strength and might of the Holy Spirit in your life. Bitterness, the direct opposite, places you in the arenas of strife, envy, revenge, confusion, illness and double-mindedness. Bitterness is a never-ending cycle that will eventually *take* your life. Forgiveness will *give* you life. Forgiveness keeps you in the Spirit and causes you to win *every time*. Don't fall into the trap of bitterness, my friend. See beyond the offenses, though they may be many, and soar in the Spirit. That's the first step to victory.

Pride Will Corrupt

The next thing we must guard against to effectively go through an attack is *pride.*

Sometimes when we have been "hit" with feeling worthless or rejected, we have a tendency to counterreact by exalting ourselves. When we do this, we are in great danger.

How can the enemy *trick* us into pride when we think we are serving God?

I have seen minister after minister fall to this deception. They have been repeatedly "hit" by the attacks of the enemy in their doctrine, their stand for God and in their personal lives. As a result, instead of staying pliable to the correcting voice of the Lord, they develop a shell of pride and enter into what I call "the persecution complex." They think they are right no matter what comes their way. If you disagree with them, they think you have a devil. They think everyone is "out to get them." Instead of hearing the voice of the Lord, they submit to a lifestyle of constant and *self-induced* persecution. In their defense, they will even pervert Scripture. They "go across the line" and eventually think if you are not under *constant* attack, you are doing nothing for God.

A "persecution complex" will cause us to do flakey spiritual things. It causes us to go into isolation and think every one and every thing is a devil. We can get a hardness about us and think it is the strength and boldness of the Lord. That pride will take us into the next phase: "the confrontation complex."

Confronting is good and it is godly. It has its place and we cannot be afraid of it. It is a *part* of the Gospel. But confronting is abused when we shove obnoxious boldness and exaggerated lifestyles on people. Confronting must only come from the **unction** of the Spirit; **not the emotion** of a groomed personality. Only pride, that has seasoned itself from hurts and wounds, causes "persecution and confrontation complexes." It deceives us into thinking we are winning and gaining ground, when in reality we are losing steadily the glory of God in our lives.

Many spiritual calls and destinies have been aborted from this area of pride. Instead of effectively going through the attack, this pride causes them to take a side road and fall prey to it.

It may be true that you are seasoned and mature. You may know many things according to the Word of God. But you must know it in the Spirit, and feed what you know by the laws of the Spirit. **To be effective, you must be strong in all areas of the Word, and not just a portion of it.** Specializing and emphasizing just a portion of the Word, feeding on those truths alone and refusing to humble yourself to the whole counsel will cause you to fall. We cannot point a finger at the world and pervert a spiritual truth by thinking we are absolutely "invincible." We cannot arrogantly attack everything that hits us and not hear the voice of the Lord first and foremost. **It may be our own correction that will cause us to win in the battle.**

To effectively go through an attack, you must examine your heart, your life, your trust and your focus in order to win and stay accurate.

Kathryn Kuhlman was constantly attacked in her ministry, from religious leaders, friends, the media and a personal mistake. She never reacted in pride. She never took on a "persecution complex" although she had natural reason to do so. Even in the time she personally stumbled, she regained her strength in a way that should teach us all. Her ministry retained such a presence of God that even when she walked into the California studios, her presence could be felt. Despite the multitudes healed and saved in her services, no one left looking at Miss Kuhlman. God took her from glory to glory, worldwide, despite the persecution and attacks.

The basic principle remains the same. Miss Kuhlman said over and over in her ministry, "I know where I came from, and I know better than anyone else what makes this ministry what it is. It's certainly not Kathryn Kuhlman."

That's the way we have to be. We make ourselves available to be used of God, despite the attacks. It is not our ability nor our intellect that works the victory. **It is the working of the Holy Spirit through a clean vessel that accomplishes it.**

James wrote to give us another foundation to effectively win in the battle:

...God resisteth the proud, but giveth grace unto the humble.

Submit yourselves therefore to God. Resist the devil and he will flee from you.

James 4:6

We must stay hooked into the Vine (John 15). We must not think we are a "special breed" because we are anointed and called. "Special breeds" die early because they unhook from the Vine. They are deceived into thinking they have all the nutrients they need. They get out on their own with what (little) they know, and they fall. Stay grafted into the Vine. The Vine gives the boldness, strength and victory you need to come forth in accuracy and progression.

Once we have realized that our true enemy is not in the natural, and we have rid ourselves of pride, then we can effectively go through a battle, use our weapons and win.

Weapon # 1

The Apostle Paul writes in Ephesians 6:13:

Wherefore take unto you the whole armor of God, that ye may be able to withstand in the evil day, and having done all, to stand.

There are several words in that Scripture that denotes action on your part. No matter how beat up and drained you feel, if you have understood the principles we just discussed, your heart will be in position for action.

Strong's Concordance says the Greek interpretation for the word "take" means **strength.*** It describes the word from the root of another word insinuating the same strength, "as the thrust of a ram."*

We could say the verse this way: "Gather a thrusting strength to yourself through the Word of God, so you may be able to oppose an attack by overcoming it and establishing yourself."

Acquaint yourself with the Word of God, your armor, in the areas of faith, truth, healing, deliverance, prosperity,

---

Strong's Concordance #142

salvation, joy, peace and soundness. The only thing that wounds the enemy is the Sword of the Spirit, or the Word of God (Ephesians 6:14-17). The Word must be strong in you. It is your security. The anointing of God can help fix your problems; but the Word of God keeps it fixed.

You must choose to believe. Hebrews 10:35 says:

> *Cast not away therefore your confidence, which hath great recompense of reward.*

The Word of God is your confidence. If you will cling to it and make it a part of you, the reward will be great. When it comes down to a brutal attack, then you must fight against it with brutal trust. The devil will try to tell you that God is not going to do anything for you and you're not going to make it. Choose to believe God and His Word. You must make a conscious choice to keep your confidence and to not cast away what belongs to you. Don't wait for an emotional outburst. Don't wait for a personal prophecy or a minister to come through and lay hands on you. Don't wait for a visit from heaven. **Just choose to believe.** I know it is hard sometimes, but God didn't call us "weak-kneed babies." He called us, "soldiers." **Get in there and believe the Word!**

You've got to be aggressive with the Word of God and allow it to work for you. Christians that keep waiting will never receive what is theirs. Ruthlessly believe the Word of God. Run out to meet it. Don't live by sovereign acts; live by faith.

What does it mean to live by faith during an attack? **It means to do, to walk, to journey.** Faith causes destiny to form and come to you. If all you can do at this point is read a verse and say, "God, I believe that," **then do it**. That is aggressive faith. Sometimes just a "string" of belief will keep you going. Don't feel guilty about that. God accepts you and will come to your aide if you will believe. It doesn't matter if the devil has come and stolen almost everything you have; **you still have something left.** If you are doing all that you can, then keep doing it. New strength will come and you will win.

Holding to the Word is not complicated; it is the will to dig into it that is hard under an attack. Just remember, no matter what it looks like in the natural, if you will hold to that thread of belief until more strength comes, you'll make it. Faith is not 3,000 confessions. Sometimes there's just enough time to say, "I believe" and swing on that cord.

Do not let the enemy speak lies to your mind. Fire back at him with the accurate scriptures you know. We shut the mouths of lions with the Word of God. Instead of a roar, you'll hear a whimpering retreat. The devil is afraid of the strength in the Spirit. So, scare him! When more strength comes to you, then learn to use more of the Word.

When you unite yourself with the Word of God, He can effectively use the rest of His weapons of war through you.

Weapon # 2

With the Word of God in me, these next scriptures are the ones I use to survive a spiritual war. These scriptures will keep you strong in God if you do what they say.

In Ephesians 5, beginning in verse 18, Paul says:

And be not drunk with wine, wherein is excess; but be filled with the Spirit;

Speaking to yourselves in psalms and hymns and spiritual songs, singing and making melody in your heart to the Lord.

Paul is encouraging us to stay filled with the Spirit.

If we stay filled with God, it will keep us in strength and joy despite what is going on around us.

How do you stay filled? He tells us: speaking to your-selves in psalms, hymns, and spiritual songs. Then sing and make melody to them and to Him.

If we go back into the Old Testament, we will find 150 psalms that tell of a man's experience with God. We find every situation that David went through, and how God delivered him from them all and showed Himself strong. David sang most of these to himself or to the Lord, and they caused him to be lifted and strengthened. The Psalms are explicit in describing the way we can feel about certain situations without condemnation. **It's called "being real with God."** Every time we are real with God and cry out to Him, He shows His strength to us.

David would say, "Lord, the devils, or these enemies are all about me, ready to consume my flesh." Or, "God, this friend I trusted in wants to take my life." Or, "Break the bones of your enemies, O God." Then he would sing, "Bless the Lord, O my soul, for You are very great." Or, "I will sing of mercy and judgment, unto you Lord will I sing." Or, "As the hart pants for water, so my soul longs for you, O God."

He was singing those words from his heart as a melody. The spirit man makes those words, and as they flow out of you, give them to God. When you do that, you will begin to make songs that will encourage your own heart and help you out.

The Psalms, just like the rest of the Word, has a continual anointing upon them. I've written several down that have ministered to me. Sometimes, I put my own melody to them from my spirit.

Sometimes, because they are in me so deeply, they come out when I least expect it. I'll be through with a meeting, standing there looking at everyone, and all of a sudden out will burst this song that had been in my heart.

One of my staff would look at me and say, "Where did that come from?" I have learned to say, "It's good! Let it go." Those songs come from your spirit to give you life and encouragement.

Through your spirit, the Holy Spirit will witness and speak to you. Many times, when you are singing to God, He will begin to sing right out of you and give you an answer. Have you ever had that?

I can remember when I was in my worst war, those songs would start way down deep in me. They would be just a small little voice. I kept giving place to it and by the end of the day, it would come out real bold. I would sing on my bed. Sometimes, even when I would ache, the songs of the Spirit would still come. I would sing for hours. I would say over and over, "God, I believe in You." It didn't matter what was happening around me. Sometimes, I would write the things that were inside of me out on paper. That's what David and others did in the Psalms. They wrote the melodies inside of them for others to see and receive life. That's what hymns are. Written melodies from hearts crying out and rejoicing to God, proclaiming Him as Lord despite the battles.

Don't be afraid to pour your heart out to God. Cleansing comes when we do that. The devil tells you, "If you say what you really feel, that is doubt." God understands you and knows how you feel anyway. Sometimes you have to have that release to get the garbage out of you. You have to say, "God, here it comes, but I still believe." Remember that and let it go.

Sometimes as a believer, we can get so caught up in the mechanics of faith we forget the character of God. In all of your journeyings, in all of your battles, in all of your situations, always remember when you come to Jesus, He receives. He doesn't cast you out. No matter where you are, no matter what you look like, if you come believing, you are accepted. The mercy and strength of God will restore you back to where you belong.

When we make melody from our hearts, life will come from heaven and keep you going. If we don't have life, we don't win. God will move for you, but sometimes we have to "prime the pump." Do you know what I mean by that? Go over into the Book of Psalms, and let those anointed words carry you out into the blessedness of the Spirit. Then, just catch up to it and sing your own songs.

You may say, "Well, I just don't know if that is necessary."

If Paul encouraged us to do it; Moses and Miriam did it as they saw the victory; and David did it when he was in the midst of war, then those are just three big examples we need to learn from and practice today. When your church is in a war, when you are under attack and feel you are getting weak, then one thing you need to do is let the songs of the Spirit come out of your mouth. Let them soar and sing them loud. Don't be embarrassed. Your own ears need to hear it!

Make your head take account. Make your head line up and listen to what your Spirit is saying. Your whole war may just be in your head; and the words of the Spirit will soothe the mental part of man. Words can soothe or disturb. The songs of the Spirit will cause peace to come into a disturbed mind, a disturbed flesh and a disturbed heart. Songs of the Spirit cause peace in the midst of a great storm. They will give you the strength to continue and win in the battle. These melodies will bring your soul back into common sense so it can be renewed. They restore your position in the spirit.

Praise and worship is a "traveling vehicle." It will cause you to travel into the good things of the Lord. It causes you to have an understanding of the greatness, the Almightiness, and the awesomeness of God. When we sing and worship from our hearts, He comes down (John 4). Praise and worship is a balance for you during attack.

Many times during a battle, it seems as if God is nowhere. These kinds of songs will give you a God-consciousness and keep you from being totally devil-conscious. In other words, as much as you are under attack, you must worship to stay accurate.

You don't have to wait to go to church where there are musical instruments. You don't have to have a music leader. You do exactly what the Scripture says. You make music in your heart, by yourself. It may sound dead and dry. If that discourages you, then go back to the Book of Psalms and read some more. Stay there and let it put your heart in position. Pretty soon, you will begin to get encouraged and songs will come out of you. You'll sing about your situation, about all the problems, and many times the Lord will sing out the answer.

The songs of the Lord are a weapon. They stop the condemnation and onslaught of the enemy in your life.

I remember many years ago, I took my first trip to Africa. I was in the nation of Mozambique and it was a communist country. They were in war and didn't like Americans too well. But I felt led of the Lord to go, so I obeyed and went.

I had felt in my spirit that there was going to be some type of military action and it came to me so strongly, that I knew it would happen. I had thought that it would be on the way into the country.

As I entered in from Zimbabwe, I saw all kinds of buildings that had been blown up. I just sat there and continued to pray protection scriptures over myself.

There was no mishap, and I preached in a little grass hut Assembly of God church that night. As a matter of fact, I slept in the church when the service was over. The next day everything was going in a normal manner. I thought, "Well, maybe my meditation and praying stopped everything. Maybe I was supposed to pray and prevent."

So, I forgot about it and climbed in the back of an old truck taking me back to Zimbabwe.

As I began to sleep in the back of that truck, gun fire woke me up. Someone yelled, "Get out of the truck!" Well, being as young as I was at the time, I stood up and looked around. Not being used to that kind of situation, I thought the bullets flying over my head had to be meant for someone else — not me!

By the grace of God, I finally realized those bullets were meant for my body and my life and I had better take some natural covering. So I got in a ditch and laid down and prayed. A good part of this story is that I was not afraid. The reason was, up to that time, John Wayne movies were about the extent of my military awareness! I didn't really know what was going on and how dangerous it actually was. I remember telling my angels if I died, they were getting it on the way up!

When the encounter ended, several people had been shot and some died. We got back in the truck, and it was then that I got scared.

As I started again on the way to Zimbabwe, I just began to worship and pray to ease myself. I kept saying to the Lord, "I thought a good man's steps were ordered by the Lord. Did I miss it?"

As I sat there and kept plugging heaven for an answer, it suddenly came back to me. I remember it as clear as yesterday.

It seemed as if a little breeze came to me and I began to sing for half an hour or more. I sang in tongues for awhile.

There are times when you can sing in tongues by choice and times you can sing in your natural language by choice. But there are also times that the Spirit will unction you, and it comes out of you in both tongues and natural language. You can tell the difference. It has more force to it when it comes by the Spirit. It "booms" out of you.

When the gifts of the Spirit come to you this way, you don't have to have someone to interpret. You can interpret yourself.

That's what happened to me that day. As I began to sing, the Lord began to speak right out of me. He began to speak the answer and the causes back to me. He told me of His protection and His reasons.

See, that song came right up out of me and satisfied my soul, my flesh and my spirit. I was at peace with what happened that day, and it never bothered me again.

When melodies come from your heart, they will come in a perfect flow, rhythm and all. Sometimes you'll say words you didn't even know how to say before. It's fun to hear how the Spirit orchestrates and causes the words to rhyme. Do you know why it's fun? Because it produces life.

Begin to enter into the songs from your heart. They will put you in remembrance of how great God is. As you sing these kinds of songs, God will be bigger to you than any problem you face. They will produce great joy and as a result, great strength.

Weapon #3

Once you have opened your heart to God, it will be easy to do what James 5:15 says

> *Confess your faults one to another, and pray for one another, that ye may be healed. The effectual fervent prayer of a righteous man availeth much.*

Another way to say that verse is, "Once you have forgiven one another, then the unceasing prayer that is united spirit, soul and body will prevail over circumstances and be of much strength."

Sometimes we focus so keenly on the latter part of that verse, we forget the first part of it.

If your attack has come through another person, you must forgive the person and their actions. No matter how hard it seems now, begin to speak forgiveness out of your mouth. If you are strong in your purpose and intent, your heart will soon follow the words you speak. According to this verse, it is only *after* we forgive that our prayers can be effectual and fervent, availing much. How can a prayer be heard by God and produce great results, if it is prayed from a heart filled with bitterness and revenge? If you have purposely filled yourself with the Spirit of God (Weapon #2), then there is no room for offense and bitterness.

It doesn't matter how feeble you feel or how weak your words start out. Remember, Jesus never turns you away, because *He hears your heart* over your words. God is not complicated. When you're under attack, any prayer you offer to God (supported spirit, soul and body) will produce results if your heart desires His will. Sometimes we think we have to groan and travail for hours to get a result. If you have the strength to do that under attack, and are led by His Spirit, by all means do it.

But we have to be careful in our definition of prayer to keep "religion" out of it. Prayer is simply talking to God. It is not a formula or a ritual. I like what my grandmother says when people come to her and say that can't pray. She answers, "Well, you can talk to your father, can't you? Talk to God the same way." When I was under my heaviest attack, I knew that even my thoughts toward God counted as a prayer to Him.

Fervent prayer produces results. What do I mean by fervent? We have three parts to our being: spirit, soul and body. Jesus said in Matthew 12:25:

And Jesus knew their thoughts, and said unto

them, Every kingdom divided against itself is brought to desolation; and every city or house divided against itself shall not stand.

As individuals, we are a "kingdom" consisting of a spirit, soul and body. Therefore, you are not a mind. You are a *spirit* that owns a *mind* that lives in a *body*.

If these three parts of your "kingdom" are divided, you'll fall. If your mind is planning your next business venture, party or vacation, your body wants to go to sleep and your spirit is not leading them, you're divided. That is not a prayer that is fervent and it will not see results.

Prayer during an attack starts from the same source as any other spiritual arena: it comes by choice. It takes what I call "willpower" to grab hold of all three parts and make yourself go into prayer concerning your situation.

During a spiritual attack, chaos hits. Everything, both inside and outside of you, is out of order. It takes an active decision on your part to pull yourself back in line.

A person who has not made that decision will face three different directions. He won't know which way to go or what to believe. He can go the body way, and try to forget his problems through the flesh. Or he can go the mind way, and live in paranoia and confusion. Or, he can choose the spirit's way, and pull everything back in its proper arena.

Spiritual attacks will paralyze you. They try to frighten you by worry and fear, frustrating you into doing nothing. As a result, your body will not obey you, your mind will talk you out of or into whatever comes its way, and you'll fall. A kingdom divided cannot stand. *The devil defeats you by dividing you.*

Fervent does not mean "scared faith." Scared faith is a little bit of fear mixed with a little faith. God didn't say that *scared faith* works; He said *fervent* prayer works.

In an attack, it doesn't matter how small your faith may seem; just stay fervent in it. Don't be overwhelmed by the entire situation around you; just stick to one thing at a time. The mind cannot properly focus on a variety of things at one time. Fervent prayer is focused. It is prayer that believes. Start with the most important thing to you, the first priority; and fervently pray and believe God for the answer and the help. It doesn't matter if all the details of the situation are intertwined. Start with the most important detail and stick to that one. The answer will come, because you will have the faith to believe for it. As soon as the peace comes, then move on to deal with the next situation.

When you pray under an attack, don't be frustrated if it feels like your prayer only hits the ceiling. Just have enough faith to believe God reached down and got it.

If we get condemned by thinking our prayers didn't go anywhere, it will make us quit. Remember that any amount of faith goes a long way, even if you do not feel at your highest or best.

When you are under a heavy spiritual attack, you are limited by your natural language. God has made a help for us in times of trouble; He is the Holy Spirit.

Likewise the Spirit also helpeth our infirmities (weaknesses); for we know not what we should pray for as we ought; but the spirit itself maketh intercession for us with groanings which cannot be uttered.

And he that searcheth the hearts knoweth what is the mind of the spirit, because he maketh intercession for the saints according to the will of God.

Some have misinterpreted this scripture as referring to our own human spirit or our own mind. Our own mind is limited and cannot always speak what is accurate. This text is referring to God's Holy Spirit that dwells inside the believer. The Holy Spirit is always there to lead us into the correct answer.

The Bible tells us that He will come to our aide, energize us, and pray through us to the perfect will of God in the situation. In Strong's Concordance, the Greek interpretation for intercession means: "Superior to, very chiefest, very highly, of necessity, to reign.*"

Strong, spiritual tongues have a place in the believers life. The scriptures say that when we have said everything we know to say from our natural minds, the Spirit Himself will pray the highest form of prayer through us by words that cannot be articulated. The Spirit of God knows the will of God in every situation. When we allow Him to pray through us, the correct answer comes to our spirit; and our mind can interpret it and know what to do.

Groanings of the spirit can only come by the Spirit's unction; **not** from a preplanned emotion. The Bible speaks in Exodus of God answering and delivering the people as He heard their groanings. But these *human* groanings of grief and despair were only *symbolic* of the manifestation of the Spirit of God in the Book of Romans. We must be careful not to get into works of the flesh when we deal with a spiritual situation. The Spirit of God is ready and willing to link up with you and pray the perfect will of God in every situation.

The cleansing of our hearts, the Word of God, the knowledge and understanding of what strong prayer can do, will lead us into total victory every time.

Believe that your angels will work on your behalf. Hebrews 1:14 speaks of our angels and says:

Strong's Concordance #5228

Are they not all ministering (serving) *spirits, sent forth to minister for them who shall be heirs of salvation?*

In Matthew 4:11, when the attack against Jesus was over, the Bible says the angels came and ministered to Him. As an heir through Jesus Christ, angels are also assigned to us. Use every weapon God has provided for you and win the battle, in Jesus' Name.

Chapter 4

The Soul Under Attack

There is one great rule we must always remember: *Wounds left unattended attract evil spirits.*

In the natural, whenever an animal is badly wounded, vultures follow it, circle it, and when the animal is down, they attack and eat their prey. These dumb and skimpy birds did nothing to cause the downfall of their prey; they just take advantage of it and help it die. The same is true in the spirit realm.

When a hurt or wound is left unattended, in any area of our lives, it attracts the enemy. He will follow you, circle you and aggravate you, until that hurt causes your downfall. If it is not dealt with, he will "feed" upon it until you are consumed. Many have left the ministry, left their mates, or left their destiny because they did not recover from a hurt.

You cannot play with hurts and wounds. You can't pretend they will go away if you don't think about them. Hurts and wounds that have not been attended to, are the primary cause of believers who need deliverance. Although a believer *cannot* be possessed in their spirit, they can go through similar stages in their soul and body. Those stages are: *oppression, depression and obsession.*

There is a war against the soul of man.

The main problem of this decade will not be the fear of

war, the AIDS epidemic, or the homeless. The number one problem of this decade will be mental illness. There will be a great struggle for the soul of man. Even as we look around the world today, there is a war for the minds of the people.

Even the media has discerned this problem. Toothpaste and orange juice commercials used to corner the market. Now we continually see ads for help with abuse and mental problems. There is one ad that shows a nice looking young man lying on his bed at home. His parents walk in and scream something like this, "Why can't you work? Why can't you get up and go to school? What's your problem, you lazy person?" Then the announcer comes on and says, "He's not physically ill. He is mentally ill. If you are like this or know someone who is, call this toll-free number." What's happening to our world? We're in a struggle over the soul of man.

Two Devices

According to Scripture, there are two devices used to thwart the soul of man. First Peter 2:11 says:

> **Dearly beloved, I beseech you as strangers and pilgrims, abstain from fleshly lusts, which war against the soul.**

One problem that wars against the soul of man is the lust of the flesh. The "natural arena," or lust of the flesh, is bountiful in the world today. I call it the natural arena, because these attacks come by things we can explicitly see with our natural eyes. Many have paid a serious price in their soul for being deeply involved with it. The good news is that no problem is too big or too ugly for God to heal and make right.

The second problem that wars against the soul of man

takes place in the "spiritual arena." It takes the Word and the maturing of our inner man to fight these attacks, because in the spiritual arena, we cannot see with our natural eyes. The consequence of these attacks remains unseen, unless we are alerted by our inner man. This area, where the devil wars his main attack, will be the focus of our discussion.

The spiritual arena has often been camouflaged and ignored. This is mainly due to our ignorance on how to effectively overcome the problems we don't understand. In Matthew 22:37, Jesus admonished a Pharisee by saying:

> *Thou shalt love the Lord thy God with all thy heart, and with all thy soul, and with all thy mind.*

This exhortation clearly shows the arenas the enemy attacks. If our enemy can keep our soul preoccupied and tormented, then we are unable to fulfill the plan of God for our lives. Maintaining a clear and free soul opens the door for the love of God in us. As a result, His purpose can be fulfilled through us.

Third John 2 states:

> *Beloved, I wish above all things that thou mayest prosper and be in health, even as thy soul prospereth.*

It is true that our spirit is perfect, complete and mature through Jesus Christ. But the affect we have on the earth is determined by the prospering of our soul.

Arenas of the Human Soul

The soul of man has often been misunderstood in the Church, and is usually ignored. There is an element of fear in the believer when it comes to understanding the soul.

God created every part of the soul of man, and we must replace the fear of it by the truth of the Word in order to understand it. God meant for every part of our being to be used to its greatest potential.

There are five key areas to the human soul: **The will, the emotions, the intellect, the imagination and the memory.**

All five of these areas were created by God and designed to be maintained and used according to the Word of God. Each area of our soul is to be generated by our spirit. The Holy Spirit, through our spirit man, should inspire and influence our will, our emotions, our intellect, our imagination and our memory.

Unless we understand how the enemy attacks our soul, the desire of the Spirit will not manifest through us. When we have an unharnessed soul, the desires of it will be the dominating factor in our lives.

Although our spirit is secure the minute we are born-again, **our soul is being constantly renewed.** In the Book of Philippians, Paul exhorts us to, *"work out our own salvation"* (2:12). In other words, we are to constantly renew our soul with the Word of God and stand against the attacks upon it.

When an attack hits, the spirit man always bounces back faster than the soul. The soul must learn to regroup and strengthen itself through the Word of God. Sitting under strong, anointed preaching helps to line up your soul. Accurate praise and worship also effects the soul to pursue God and win.

We have the ability to understand our will, our emotions, intellect, imagination, memory and to walk by maturity through each one. We can possess our whole man. If you are fighting a battle in your soul, purpose in your heart to win in it. Neutrality in any form spells defeat. We must move forward *internally* before an outward manifestation is seen. **An internal security will always produce an outward stability.**

In the following chapters, we will discuss the five areas of the soul as well as the spiritual attacks against each one.

Chapter 5

The Will Under Attack

The will is the dominant force of the human soul. It doesn't matter if you are born-again or not, **the human will has the final say in any decision.**

God created humankind with a will. He doesn't want robots to love and serve Him. He receives pleasure from the choice we make with our will to serve Him. Our praise and worship delights Him, because it comes from a choice to do it.

It is our decision if we go to heaven or hell. God didn't make the Lake of Fire for us. It was made for the devil and his angels; but we can go live and burn there forever if we choose to. Heaven is made for those who love God and want to live with Him. It's that simple.

It is our choice if we serve God or the devil. It is our decision if we give into sin or live in purity. Even after we are born-again, it is our decision if we experience the things of God or just, "go to church on Sunday." Even when the call to ministry comes, it is still your decision to accept it or reject it.

The human will is sovereign. God will not violate it. We cannot make wrong decisions and then blame God for the outcome. Responsibility comes with the human will. Those who refuse to be responsible and choose to live however they please, prefer to blame God for their trouble and calamity. But He is not responsible for our choices — **we are.**

Function of the Will

How can you know the working of the human will over the rest of the soul? Let me give you an example everyone can relate to.

Let's say that you've just finished a huge meal and dessert is being brought to the table. Your mother has just made your favorite chocolate cake and you know you shouldn't eat another bite.

Suddenly, your *imagination* comes in and you think, "I just know that creamy fudge icing is heaped an inch think on that cake." Your *memory* cites in, "Remember how rich and moist that cake is? Remember how great it tasted last Christmas?" The *emotions* chide, "You know how much fun we have eating mom's chocolate cake together. We can laugh and talk and have a good time!" Your *mind* begins to signal the rest of your body; your *eyes* focus on the cake, your *mouth* begins to water, your *stomach* is full but says, "I'll make room!" and out of nowhere **the will** steps in and shouts, **"NO!"**

That ends it right there. The rest of your soul and body rebels, but your will made a decision and that's the **final word.** Every other part of you has to line up to whatever the will says.

That's a fun illustration, but it helps us identify the other parts of our soul and helps us to see the importance of our will. The same is true in the spirit realm. When the rest of our soul wants to get out of line, the will has the authority to bring us back on track. That's why it doesn't matter how you feel in order to gain a result. You will always feel either up or down, but the will is your mainstay. *Your will always makes the final decision,* wrong or right. Your will is the strongest part of your soulish being.

When our will is obedient to the Word and the Spirit of God, the rest of our soul soon follows. Our emotions are forced to feel the right way, and our mind is trained to think on the right things. **The human will is the disciplinary factor of the soul.**

The human will is not automatically born-again like the spirit is. Our mind must be *transformed* by the Word and the unction within us to serve God and fulfill His purpose on earth.

The human will begins to function before birth. As a fetus inside the mother, the baby still uses the will to move its arms and legs. Once born, it is the job of the parents to train the will of the child. When a child has a temper tantrum or similar outbursts, it is not from the emotions or the intellect. It is from an uncontrolled will that must be taught discipline and control.

When we are born-again, our will changes. The rebellion in our heart towards God can't come as easily. We now have a will to serve Him. We now have a will to do what is right and pleasing to Him. From the moment of New Birth, our will submitted to the plan of God and ceased to be our own. From that day forward, **it was intended for our will to be disciplined and trained by the Word of God.** A will seasoned by the Word will produce life, health and joy. It will always cause you to make choices that produce increase and abundance. The circumstances surrounding you will be irrelevant.

There is no greater joy than to merge the human will into the will of God. **The greatest experience on earth is knowing you have linked your will with the will of the Father.** In doing so, all of heaven is behind your every effort. The greatest strength on earth is in knowing God is pleased and walks beside you. When the human will and the will of God become as one, we are invincible. There is no foe that can stand, no attack that can conquer. There is no disease that can destroy, and no curse that can come.

The problem comes when we don't know or understand the power of our human will. However, our enemy understands our potential. He knows his defeat is sure, unless he can sway our will.

The Will of the Enemy

Just as we have a will, Satan himself has a will. God created him as a beautiful archangel, a chief musician in Heaven who led worship to the Father. But through his will, he followed the lust of pride and thought **he** would take over the Throne of God (Isaiah 14:12-14). As a result, he was kicked out of heaven like lightning (Luke 10:18). By his will, *he changed his status* from Lucifer to Satan. God didn't create Satan; He made Lucifer. **But through a choice of his will, he perverted his own destiny and is forever cursed by his choice.** He is now Satan, the enemy of God and humanity.

His demons have a will also. They willfully carry out the plans of their leader and vow to faithfully fulfill them.

In the Book of John, Chapter 10, we can read a very familiar verse that explains the will of the enemy:

> *The thief comes only in order to steal and kill and destroy...*

> *Verse 10, Amplified Version*

The goal of the enemy is to steal your will for God. In doing so, he can eventually destroy you. When our will for God is gone, poverty, sickness, disease, calamity and disaster come. Our joy and strength can be robbed from us through the lack of willpower. Passive decisions or a lack of will can even cause physical death.

Demonic Results

How does the human will go under the attack of the enemy? Through passivity and lethargy.

Passivity and lethargy are the major killers of spiritual life. Webster's defines these words as, "sluggish, inactivity; drowsy dullness."

We are to be a people who are excited, courageous, creative and enthusiastic. When we say "yes" to God, a whole new world opens up and places us on the cutting edge. New joy, life and strength come to us.

When the human will is under attack, we lose our zeal for God. Suddenly, we could care less if the Gospel is ever preached again. We become lazy, careless and slothful. Our discipline and diligence is gone.

Indecisiveness becomes the predominant factor in our lives. We can't see or hear what is wrong or right. Instead of the godly strength to produce and live by our decisions, we rely on the opinions of others. What another man **says** carries more weight than what we *know* in our hearts. If we are not careful, we end up confused and doubting, tossed by everything we hear.

How can the enemy cause a human will to become passive? **Through constant vexation, or harassment.** We must understand that the enemy very rarely hits one time. Instead he constantly, day in and day out, beats against what we stand for until we are worn out. When he has beat our will to a thread and we have not renewed ourselves by the Word of God, then one major hit will knock us out. That's why we wake up one morning and find ourselves in sin. That's why we look around one day and find our marriages in shambles. That's why some marry the wrong person. It's because their will was made weak through constant vexation.

The Will of Samson

Let's look at a biblical example of a strong will made weak by the enemy.

In the thirteenth chapter of the Book of Judges, there was a man born of great physical strength named Samson. This man had a great destiny. Before his birth, an angel appeared to his mother and said that her son would begin to deliver the Israelites from the enemy. This angel also told her the factors of his strength and what he must do in order to perform the will of God for his people.

Samson had a wonderful childhood. Scripture tells us that the Spirit of the Lord would come upon him many times during his youth. He once tore a lion apart with his bare hands, and slew a thousand men with the jawbone of a donkey.

But Samson had one problem; he loved the women of the world and chose them over the women of God.

Because Samson did not follow the Word of God for his life, he opened the door for the enemy to destroy him. Samson's strength was directly linked to his will. Had his will been submitted to God, he would have been invincible. He would have not only had physical strength, but the spiritual strength to say, "No!" when the enemy came. But through repeated sinful pleasures, his human will was weakened by a stronger human will: the will of Delilah.

The Philistines were the enemies of the people of God. They had kept the people of God in bondage for years. The only wall between them and the Israelites was the strength of their leader, Samson.

The Philistines reasoned that they could only capture Samson through the woman he loved. No physical strength could capture him. No army had been able to contain him. So they approached Delilah and offered her a bribe. Her job was to make Samson tell her the secret of his strength. Because she was from the camp of the enemy and her love for money was stronger than her love for Samson, she obliged.

Three different times she whined and begged Samson

to tell her his secret. Although he tricked her those three times, his will was becoming weaker and weaker. Finally, the fourth time came:

> *And she said unto him, Howst can thou say, I love thee, when thine heart is not with me? Thou hast mocked me these three times, and hast not told me wherein thy great strength lieth.*
>
> *And it came to pass, when she pressed him daily with her words, and urged him, so that his soul was vexed unto death;*
>
> *That he told her all his heart...*
>
> *Judges 16:15-17*

Samson's will was pressed and vexed until he succumbed. As a result, he was robbed of his strength and taken into captivity. In the end, as he cried out for the mercy of God, more Philistines were killed than ever before, but Samson died with them.

As believers, we must fight for and protect our will for God. As we deeply plant the Word of God into our will, the plan of God is easier to follow. With the Word as our substance, it is easier to stand against the schemes of the enemy. When controversy comes, we will have the strength to shout, "No!" in the face of trouble.

That kind of strength is what Ephesians 6 talks about in part. It says:

> *Wherefore take unto you the whole armor of God, that ye may be able to withstand in the evil day, and having done all, to stand.*
>
> *Verse 13*

Although our own strength *alone* accomplishes nothing, our will fused into the will of God enables us to stand through any attack the enemy brings. Our human will can only be strengthened through the Word of God. When God's will is joined with our will, we will not wear out under pressure. Godly strength produces endurance and patience.

Outwardly, our physical strength can only stand for so long. It is possible to perform certain feats for God in your own physical strength, but they will not last. Remember that, "inward security produces outward stability." When the inner man is strong, the will latches onto it. As a result, the works we do for God will be lasting and have great effect in the earth.

I've seen many strong men and women fall into the trap of relying on their own strength for the ministry. They get so caught up in the works of God, they fail to renew themselves and keep their inner man strong. It comes to the point that they are unable to discern between their own physical strength and the strength of God through them. Sadly, the works they accomplish fall away and become a spectacle to believers and sinners alike.

Your physical strength, or human will, cannot fight spiritual battles without the strength of God.

I must also point out that we are not to confuse the gifts of God, or the anointing, with the strength of God. Just because we may have an anointing from God to heal the sick does not mean our will is linked with God's will. Do not confuse the two, because the gifts from God are another subject entirely. We have a responsibility to build up our inner man through the Word of God, **inspite of our accomplishments,** great or small.

I've told this story before, but it is worth telling again. In my grandparents' day, there was a minister greatly used in the gifts of God. He had such a powerful anointing that all he had to do was raise his hand, and everyone in the prayer line would be slain in the spirit at once. Many healings took place. Yet he ran off with one of the women in the church and divorced his wife. It really bothered me that something like that could happen.

What was the problem? He had a weak will. He had not taken the time to build his inner man and make it strong. When the attack of the enemy came, he fell and caused countless others to slander the Gospel. *He relied on his gift as his strength.* The gifts are "extra" my friend. **Where the rubber meets the road is in whether or not your human will is merged with the will of God, in every situation.** The "whole armor of God" or the principles of the Word of God, MUST be grafted to your own will.

In this decade, God is requiring more from us as leaders and believers. Maturity and discernment must come forth from the Body of Christ. God will require an answer for our accomplishments, whether they were lasting and accurate, or weak and failing. Our goal should be a lasting accomplishment; not a "spiritual explosion" for the moment.

The Will of Joseph

We saw how Samson, through his weakened will, fell during an attack of the enemy. His accomplishments were short-lived. I've said in many of my meetings, had Samson developed a stronger inner man and learned by his will to say "No!" , the Book of Judges would have been longer. He would have accomplished more for the Kingdom of God and there would have been more to write about. Instead, we can learn a sad but important message from his life.

But there is also a great lesson to be learned from a man named Joseph. Although Joseph made minor mistakes in the beginning of his call, **he learned from them and turned them into godly strength.** He was faced with a similar situation; but the inner strength he had developed caused his will to remain strong and fixed with God's will.

In the 39th chapter of the Book of Genesis, we begin reading the area I want to illustrate.

Joseph had been sold in slavery to an Egyptian officer named Potiphar. Because the inner man of Joseph was strong, God prospered him and caused great favor to be upon him. Potiphar trusted him and promoted him as overseer of his entire household.

This is where the enemy likes to operate. **He will wait, many times, until great favor and recognition comes to us before he launches his greatest attack.** If we have not prepared our inner man, we can be caught up in the glory and workings of it all, and fall into his schemes. This is where many strong leaders have fallen.

We can begin reading of the attack in verse seven:

And it came to pass after these things, that his master's wife cast her eyes upon Joseph; and she said, Lie with me.

But he refused, and said unto his master's wife, Behold, my master wotteth not what is with men in the house, and he hath committed all that he hath to my hand;

There is none greater in this house than I; neither hath he kept back any thing from me but thee, because thou art his wife: how then can I do this great wickedness, and sin against God?

Notice that Joseph's will was strong against this wrong. But one initial response doesn't shake the enemy. He continued his attack against Joseph, hoping to weaken his human will and cause him to fall. The enemy continued to harass and torment Joseph through this woman, hoping to wear out his will.

And it came to pass, as she spake to Joseph

day by day, that he hearkened not unto her, to lie
by her, or to be with her.

Verse 10

Had Joseph's will not been fused with the will of God, this vexation would have caused him to fall. But Joseph was strong with the Word of God and in the next verses we will see what he did to prove it:

And it came to pass about this time, that
Joseph went into the house to do his business;
and there was none of the men of the house there
within.

And she caught him by his garment, saying, Lie
with me: and he left his garment in her hand, and
fled, and got him out.

Verse 11, 12

Joseph showed his inner strength by running away from the trouble. He was not cowardly in his action. He showed the enemy who was in control.

Years ago, the Spirit of God showed me that part of learning to "run the race" was *knowing when to run away and when to stay.* There is a time to run, just as there are times to stay and confront. "Running the race" of God is a spiritual art. In the New Testament, there were times when the Apostle Paul confronted; and there were times he fled the city.

In this particular instance, Joseph, in order to continue running the race, knew to run away so he could fulfill his destiny in purity. He was led by the unction of his spirit. Because his human will was immersed in the will of God, he knew *exactly* what to do.

Although the enemy falsely accused Joseph through Potiphar's wife (verses 13-20), the accusation could not stand forever. The enemy plagued Joseph the best he could, but God always wins through us when our will is submitted to Him (verse 21). In the end, Joseph was exalted in Egypt next in line to Pharaoh. He was able to forgive the brothers that sold him into slavery, nations were saved from famine and God was exalted.

Had Joseph succumbed to the attack of the enemy, his destiny would have been thwarted. Our enemy works the same today.

Demonic Attack

Spiritual attacks are targeted to gain control of our will. If our will is broken, we will fall. By making sin attractive, the enemy aims to weaken our human will and cause us to fail God and humanity.

Understand the devil cannot violate your will. He does not have the power to override it. He must have your permission to take you over. Even a non-believer has the willpower to say, "No!" to the devil.

The Holy Spirit will **never** override your human will. Instead He speaks to it, witnesses to it, instructs it. But He will never violate it. The choice is your own.

The devil, on the other hand, wants to violate and control your will. **He will wear it down by lies, tragedies, harassments and bombardments until he owns it.** If you easily yield your will over to his methods by falling prey to the circumstances he puts around you, your will weakens little by little. Before you know it, you have no strength left to fight, and he owns your will. You suddenly find yourself giving in to everything he suggests or puts before you.

If you are being pressed daily, harassed and tormented to fall into sin, then you are under a spiritual attack. The battle is over the control of your will. In order to win, you must begin to strengthen yourself through the Word of

God. Find the scriptures that deal with the trouble you are facing. Let strength and encouragement from the Word give you the courage to stand. Look at the situation squarely in the face and speak the Word of God to it. The Word of God is designed to handle the pressure. Adverse circumstances melt at the spoken Word. No matter how weak your will seems today, you are the one in control to make it stronger. Submit it to the will of God through the Word of God. **Receive what you read as a way of life.**

Let your will cause you to arise. By your will, receive the Word of God and let it walk you into nations. You can fulfill the call and destiny planned for you from the positive response of your will.

Remember that eternal consequences are far greater than the temporary trials we face. The action of your will is eternal. Fight for what God has given you, and do not bow to the temporal onslaught against you. *The moment of trouble will pass; but the decisions you make will stand forever.*

Chapter 6

The Emotions Under Attack

Just as God has given us a will, He has also given us emotions. The emotional side of humankind is a world all its own.

In the past, due to lack of knowledge, the Church was widely led by their emotions. Because of this error, many were taught it was unscriptural to feel anything, or when we do, to lie about it and say we don't. This teaching is in as much error as the previous.

The fact is, we **do** feel things in our soul, good or bad. It is not wrong to have emotions; **but it is wrong to have them out of control.** Our emotions are out of balance when we base the decisions of our life around them.

God desires for you to have emotions. He gave them to you. But we are not to use them to manipulate or control another person. We are not to use them to find the will of God for our lives. We are not to use them to prove the Spirit of God is working in our lives. Our emotions are not the basis of true love, or the lack of it.

Just as color adds life to a black and white television show, so our emotions were created to do in our individual lives. Our emotions were not made to rule us; but to enhance us. They were made to show detail and depth. They were given to us to show the personality and character of God in the earth. They were not created to be the sole expression of our being; neither were they created to remain dormant.

Just as the rest of our soul, the emotions must be matured through the Word of God. When we feel something contrary to the will of God, it is wrong. If we don't stop it there, our emotions will literally lead our lives by wrong desires. **Wrong emotions have the potential to steal your destiny for God.**

The emotional side of man, by nature, is unruly. It is an unharnessed frontier that must be conquered by the inner man. Our emotions must be steered and guided. When emotions manifest, they must have purpose behind them. When our inner man guides our emotions, great results are produced.

When our emotions are led by our spirit, it opens the door for the mercy of God to be manifest in the earth. Our emotions can show the joy of God, the grievance of the Spirit, the urgency of the hour. The emotions can express the anger of the Lord or the peace He extends to the troubled mind.

Emotional Sources

When we break it down, our emotions come from two sources: the unregenerated man, or the born-again, spirit-filled man. Our emotions are an outburst from one of the two.

When emotions come from the unregenerated part of man, they are carnal. They feel opposite from the Word of God. They want to be in control. Because the world does not understand spirit-led living, they operate entirely by their emotions and intellect. To them, it is fine to do whatever feels good. If they wake up one morning and do not feel a positive emotion for their mate, they leave them. If it feels good to have an illicit relationship, they do it. If they don't feel like showing up for work, they don't go. Their life is in constant confusion, because their emotions are always up or down.

The emotions are the same in the believer; the only difference is the spirit man has the final say in the matter, not the emotions.

As a believer, if we are ruled by our emotions, we cannot stay in communion with God. **A prayer is not answered on the basis of emotion.** Prayer is answered when it is spoken from the unction of our spirit man, according to the Word.

Our emotional realm wants to rule our lives whether we are born-again or not. When we have a personal relationship with Jesus Christ, He becomes the "rudder of our soul." When He guides us, our emotions must line up to the Word. They are not allowed to "trick us" in things contrary to Scripture. This is where the enemy attacks us as believers.

Emotional Attacks

If we have not yet learned that our emotions are subservient to our spirit, we are open territory for the attacks of the enemy.

When the enemy cannot gain entrance into our will, he will head for our emotions. If he can get our emotions to follow him, the attack will cause our will to weaken.

A sure sign of an emotional attack is in the area of self-pity.

Self pity - a sign

When we have been hurt or wounded, the emotions pull to the forefront. During an attack, our first reaction is to withdraw under fire for protection. When we withdraw, it will pull the harness off of our emotions, allowing them to rule us. When self-pity becomes the basis from which we view everything, the enemy is running havoc with us.

When self-pity rules us, our view becomes warped. We

feel that everyone is against us and no one likes us. We begin to feel that everyone else is wrong and we are right.

Self-pity moves over into arrogance, which is an area of pride. Arrogance is the soulish way of protection. Many who have been hurt, wear arrogance as a covering to hide their wounds. When we wear that false cloak, we cut off the blessings of God into our lives. We are unable to hear His voice when He prompts us to move for Him. Even if we hear Him, we cannot break out of the sheath of arrogance to be obedient. *Arrogance*

Self-pity and arrogance is only one way the enemy rules in our emotions. Remember, his plan is to ruin your destiny in the earth. **If he can render you immobile through your emotions, then your spirit cannot follow God effectively.** *Anger → strife*

Another area the enemy attacks our emotions is in anger. If we have been hurt by another and refuse to obey the Word of God, then anger can rule us.

When anger dominates your life, every action you put forth will result in strife. Revenge becomes your utmost desire. Anger causes your emotions to revert into an adverse stage. Instead of living in the righteousness, joy and peace of your spirit, emotional anger produces, "a wilderness." It causes you to feel isolated and alone. Just as in the natural wilderness, because of fear, you are moved to hurt whatever crosses your path; so it is in this emotional realm. You are only pleased if those who hurt you are hurt themselves. Anger will eat away at you like a cancer. It is never satisfied.

Anger operates in bitterness, and if we continue to let the enemy rule our emotions in this area, we will never fulfill the plan of God in the earth.

When we allow the enemy to successfully gain ground in our emotions, we act as a carnal man. The Bible says a carnal man acts as if he has never known God or His ways (Romans 1).

Our emotions are not equipped to see into the realm of the spirit. The "eyes of faith" are gone when we are led by emotion. We are only moved by what we see in the natural. **If we are only motivated by what we see in the natural, the devil will make sure we see and hear a lot.**

Emotions will cause you to look for negative support. Gossip and slander surfaces and we find ourselves in total confusion. We no longer trust anyone and would rather function our life alone. That is how the enemy keeps his hold in our emotional realm. His whole plan is to keep your will from wanting the things of God.

Emotional Freedom

How can we break out of an emotional attack? By forcing our emotions to be silent and trust the Word of God, no matter what is happening around us.

As we have previously discussed, the Book of Psalms is a great disciplinary book for the soul. Amidst trouble and calamity, David forced his emotions to be subjected to the Word of God. He continuously said phrases like, *"Oh Lord, open thou my lips; and my mouth shall show forth thy praise"; "Make me to hear joy and gladness"; "I trust in the mercy of God forever and ever"; "I will hear what God the Lord will speak: for he will speak peace to his people";* and *"Why art thou cast down, O my soul? And why art thou disquieted within me? Hope thou in God: for I shall yet praise Him, who is the health of my countenance".*

Once I understood the spiritual implication of the attack against me and the purpose of it, the Book of Psalms became an outlet for me. The words David spoke became alive as never before. Some of these same words I spoke to God for my very life, just as David did.

Notice in every scripture I just gave, David was taking control of his emotions. It didn't matter who was wrong or right in the circumstance he was dealing with. **What mattered was how David *himself* would deal with it.** The trouble outside of him was bad enough; he couldn't afford to cave in with it. David had enough wisdom to know the trouble would pass. He could take his experience and live in bitterness; or move on into wisdom and strength. We can see from his life that he chose the latter.

The situation you may face today is much the same. We all face emotional attacks. The point is, to understand the purpose and goal of the enemy. **Once you understand according to the plan of God for your life, you are in position to make your emotions line up to the Word of God.** It is easy to open anywhere in Psalms and read the correct response to a vexing attack. As you read these Psalms, begin to express them with your own cry to God. Before long, your emotions will silence themselves and your spirit will take supremacy. When that happens, you will no longer be moved by what you see. If your emotions try to tempt you, line them up with your spirit man. The enemy will have no doorway to your emotions if you seal them with the Word of God.

Chapter 7

The Intellect Under Attack

The human brain is extraordinary. No scientist or medical doctor is able to explain how a small mass of tissue can retain and understand knowledge. Human intelligence is unexplainable to science, because God created it to function in His image.

Human intelligence, in the wrong vein, can be an enemy to the works of God. Intelligence is a wonderful thing and should be sought for; but the world has made it into their "god" and used it as the sole source of survival.

To the world, intelligence places humankind in "class categories." It does not see all men as equal. If someone doesn't think the way "our class" does, then they are called uncivilized or barbarian. According to God, the very opposite is true. **God sees men according to the heart, not the intellect.**

Intelligence was placed inside of man to help him understand the workings of God and cause prosperity to abound in the earth. Mixed with the Spirit of God, intelligence accomplishes great feats. No matter what culture we are in, if we prosper in that environment, intelligence served us. For example, I doubt a city businessman could survive in the wilderness for very long. Yet, the people who lived in the wilds, outside of an office building, were labeled "incompetent." The world has widely misused their definition of intelligence.

Godly Intelligence

To the believer, intelligence works with our spirit to cause understanding. God desires to reveal Himself to us and have us know His ways. In the Book of Isaiah, chapter one, we read:

> *Come now, and let us reason together, saith the Lord: though your sins be as scarlet, they shall be white as snow; though they be red like crimson, they shall be as wool.*

> *Verse 18*

God delights in using our intelligence to understand His ways. The Hebrew interpretation for the word "reason" means to, "decide, convict.*" Our intelligence has a part to play in conviction and submission to God. The Bible says only a fool would say, "there is no God" (Psalm 14:1).

It is the will of God for a believer to season his intelligence into godly wisdom. Proverbs 19:8 says:

> *He that getteth wisdom loveth his own soul...*

From life's experiences, intelligence will turn into godly wisdom if we mature our soul according to the Word. Proverbs goes on to say that the Lord *"lays up sound wisdom for the righteous"* (2:7); and *"happy is the man that finds wisdom"* (3:13). The Bible says that the earth was formed by wisdom and its price is far beyond rubies or gold.

Godly intelligence produces peace and security. It is a safeguard from destruction and poverty.

Natural Intelligence

Natural intelligence has a resistance for God, because

Strong's Concordance #3198

it wants to rule in His place. Natural intelligence thinks it is wiser than God, and chooses to set up rules and regulations to prove it. The theory of evolution was born from an intelligent mind. It reasoned our existence far beyond the limits and came up with its own source. Any one with common sense can see the error of such a theory.

Natural intelligence has to figure everything out. It is logical to the point of disregard to anything supernatural. There are no miracles to the natural intellect. By solely relying on the natural intellect, one cannot see the purposes of God. The Gospels aren't logical; they are spiritual. Intelligence must remain submitted to the reality of God if it is to be of true and honest use.

On the other hand, many have set up religious rules and regulations for multitudes to follow. They reason that you cannot serve God unless you do such-and-such on such-and-such day. In the Bible, the Pharisees and Sadducees were good examples of intelligent men who reasoned their service of God into works alone. There was no worship and service from the heart. If an act was done contrary to tradition, it upset their intelligence and they rejected it.

Although natural intelligence has accomplished tremendous feats, it cannot be the only source we draw knowledge or truth from. Our spirit man is to be the prime function of our being. Our intelligence is to follow the leading of our spirit. The two combined will produce accuracy in every feat we attempt.

It is in this area that the enemy begins his attack on human intelligence.

Attack on Intelligence

Remember, it is the goal of the enemy to dethrone God from His rightful position in your life. He will trick you and deceive you any way he can to accomplish his goal.

How can you tell when your intelligence is being attacked?

First and foremost, logic overrides the inward witness. Then your faith and belief in God begins to fade. Sadly, most cults of the world started from a leader who was attacked in his mind and didn't recognize it.

You may be going on your way, living your life as usual, but the thoughts come, "God isn't real. There is no such thing as healing, deliverance, etc." If you listen to it, you'll begin to intellectualize every thing you see. The enemy sets you up in thinking you are being superior and objective; but you are playing the fool.

Before long, you feel cold and dead inside. You don't want to pray and you objectively criticize the Word of God, piece by piece. You certainly will not tolerate the preaching of the Gospel. You find yourself with an opposing statement for each sentence you hear from the pulpit.

If you don't fight this attack, you will begin to look at the local church as a bunch of weak, dependent, low-life people who need a crutch in life. If you've gotten to this stage, you'll find the only things that motivate you are success-oriented exhortations that stimulate your intelligence.

Common Sense

Another area of attack is in our common sense. If the devil cannot get you to question and act upon the existence of God, he'll try to throw you over into the road of no common sense.

I heard a preacher say once, "Why is it when some people get born again, they seem to throw out their common sense?"

God expects you to use common sense mixed with the promises of His Word.

For example, there are those who confess healing scriptures all day; but they go outside in sub-zero weather without a coat. They don't take care of their bodies and diet, and expect the blessings of God in the areas of healing.

Then there are those who constantly speak prosperity on themselves to others; but never look for a job. Yes, it is true that God provides for the sparrow; but even she leaves the nest to get the worm!

There are also those that have families and assume each member knows how much they are loved, simply because they are "provided for." But these people never take the time to show their expression of love and care to them. As a result, the family never knows they are truly loved. Their children turn to other things for acceptance.

Do not be deceived in the area of common sense. Do not take important details for granted. Do not look at the Word of God as a "cure all" when you have not done your part as well. The principles of God are not "magic". Instead, they are principles of "faith;" and faith means some action on your part. Godly faith, mixed with inspired action, overcomes any obstacle in your path.

How to Recover

If you are under this attack and have believed it, the first step to recovery is **repentance.** Ask the Spirit of God to make Himself real to you and show you His works. Many have told me that almost instantly, the Lord has quickened their memory of His works and they were set free.

Ask Him then to soften your hardened heart and to give you new eyes and new ears to see and hear His Word. Force yourself to be at every meeting of your church. It doesn't matter if you want to go or not — **be there.** God will see your faithfulness and it will count as righteousness to Him. One day, you will walk into the meeting and the Spirit of God will melt your heart. He will restore and solidify His ways in you and you'll leave a new person. Remember that your heart was not hardened overnight. You cultivated the attack against you for quite a while to be in such a condition. Give the Spirit of God a chance to work with you.

Begin to be involved in the outreaches of your church. You don't have to go with the evangelism team right away; work as a door greeter or book table worker. Force yourself to be friendly and reach out to the people of God.

Purpose to be vulnerable to the message from the pulpit. Ask God to show you how it applies to **your** life. He will not fail you or leave you hanging. Begin to tithe again, and support the work of God. God will prosper you and show you the work of His hand.

You must command the spirit of unbelief to leave you in Jesus' Name and have no hold on you. You must take spiritual authority over the harassing, tormenting spirits sent to vex your thoughts. God is real; and it is far better to go to heaven serving Him than to die believing He is only a crutch.

Begin to fellowship with those who are strong in the Lord. Those who walk in godly strength will not condemn your temporary weakness. They will exhort you and live a victorious life in front of you. They will "sharpen" you as you gain strength and be a balance for you. Pray for godly friends such as that. The Bible says in Psalm 119:63:

> *I am a companion of all them that fear thee, and of them that keep thy precepts.*

Surround yourself with those that fear the Lord for that is true wisdom and intelligence. Seek after *godly* intelligence. The Bible says in Psalm 111:10:

> *"The fear of the Lord is the beginning of wisdom; a good understanding have all they that do his commandments."*

You do not have to lose your destiny with God. You do not have to fall subject to the enemy through pride and a hardened heart. Recognize his attack against you and stand your ground. If Jesus tarries His coming, the generations following you will gain from your strength and determination. **You are valuable to God and His plan.**

Chapter 8

The Imagination Under Attack

The human imagination is a part of our soul, yet vastly different from the other parts. We have the ability to imagine beyond our intelligence.

For example, we can imagine something and still not intelligently put it together. We might envision a goal or a dream, and still not have the intelligence of knowing how to get there.

To me, the imagination is a very spiritual part of our soul. It is one of our most valuable assets. I love a person that has imagined a dream and puts it into action.

Our imagination has the creative ability to do anything for God. Our imagination can build creations that humanity has not yet seen.

When we do not understand the principle of imagination, we will dream our life away. Faith is not fantasy. Idle imaginations cannot produce anything — physically or spiritually.

When I was a young boy, I was aware of the call of God on my life. I would read my Bible, pray, then shut myself in my room. I had a huge map of the world on the wall. I would stand in front of it and preach to it. I would point with my finger to different places and say, "I'm coming to you!"

That was my godly imagination, envisioning the plan

of God for my life. **I didn't stop there though.** That map of the world isn't paper hanging on my wall; it is now the ground of nations I walk into.

Imagination without action in its accurate timing is fruitless. It is heartbreaking to hear the godly imagination of a person, then watch them sit and do nothing towards it. Ten years later, the person comes to you with the same vision, maybe greater; and still works at the corner store.

Imagination is a powerful force. It changes the nations, cities, churches, and communities. It originates in your thought life.

Imagination is very important to God. If you can see something in your imagination, it is within your reach. In Genesis 11:6, the Word says:

> *And the Lord said, Behold, the people is one, and they have all one language; and this they begin to do: and now nothing will be restrained from them, which they have imagined to do.*

Although this passage was from a negative vein, the principle here is the same. Because the people were of one heart, they were able to do whatever they imagined! Their imagination was unlimited to them. From this scripture we can see that our abilities have nothing to do with our intelligence. Our ability stems from our imagination and our willingness to see it accomplished in the earth.

As a matter of fact, intelligence can be a hindrance to imagination. Imagination works for those who are daring enough to believe it, and who will stop at nothing to see it work.

Imagination comes from a desire in your heart. Your imagination will reveal the hidden secrets of your heart.

Imagination of David

Although imagination is a force, it cannot produce by

itself. It cannot come about by speaking it into existence. Imagination comes about by action. Let me give you a biblical example.

In the Book of First Samuel, we read in chapter 17, the story of David and Goliath. David used the principle of imagination in his slaying of Goliath. When he went out to face the giant, he had envisioned in his head what would happen. Goliath attempted to intimidate him; but his vision was stronger than the giant's words:

> *And the Philistine said to David, Come to me, and I will give thy flesh unto the fowls of the air, and to the beasts of the field.*

> *Then said David to the Philistine, Thou comest to me with a sword, and with a spear, and with a shield: but I come to thee in the name of the Lord of hosts, the God of the armies of Israel, who thou hast defied.*

> *This day will the Lord deliver thee into mine hand; and I will smite thee and take thine head from thee; and I will give the carcasses of the host of the Philistines this day unto the fowls of the air, and to the wild beasts of the earth; and all the earth may know that there is a God in Israel.*

> *And all this assembly shall know that the Lord saveth not with sword and spear; for the battle is the Lord's, and he will give you into our hands.*

> *Verses 44-47*

David imagined it, put it into action, and it happened just that way.

Godly Imagination

What constitutes the working of a godly imagination?

Reality or unreality. We have the ability to imagine in either vein.

When a heart is submitted to the plan of God, all his imaginations are an overflow from the Spirit of God. The plan he envisions furthers the kingdom of God and turns the hearts of humankind towards heaven. **There is no self-exaltation in godly imagination.** True imagination inspired by the Spirit of God is almost humbling. Once we've seen it, it is a reality that we can never attain without the strength of God.

The Attack of Unreality

The enemy works in our imagination by getting us to exalt ourselves. These imaginations are envisioned in the same way, but find themselves in unreality. If we are not wise to their source, we can follow them and wake up in shambles.

In the Book of Genesis, chapter 3, satan used the principle of imagination on Eve. He showed her the fruit and caused her to imagine its taste and texture. He knew the fruit was forbidden to her. The unreality set in when she was told in verses 4 and 5:

...Ye shall not surely die:

For God doth know that in the day ye eat thereof, then your eyes shall be opened, and ye shall be as gods, knowing good and evil.

Her imagination in eating the fruit would make her equal with God. She envisioned it, took her husband with her, they ate it and were cursed. They fell into the trap of the enemy through their imagination.

That is what 2 Corinthians, chapter 10 is telling us:

Casting down imaginations and every high

*thing that exalteth itself against the knowledge
of God, and bringing into captivity every thought
to the obedience of Christ.*

**Imaginations that exalt themselves over the word of
God are not from heaven.**

Sometimes we are deceived into thinking that any feat
accomplished is from God. That is not true. The end results
and the lasting effects show what spirit it is of. The believer
may have had good intentions but was ignorant along the
way of the attack of the enemy.

**If the enemy cannot get us to imagine selfish dreams,
then he will try to turn those for God into self-exalting
imaginations.** You must guard against those attacks and
seek to bring God glory in everything you do.

How can we be deceived into self-exalting imaginations? There are several reasons. One is in the area of pride.
Another in the area of undisciplined flesh. Still another, in
the area of hurts and wounds.

But a point I want to bring out is in the area of fantasy.

The world offers a variety of creative fantasy. In this
troubled generation, multitudes are searching for a way to
escape the pressure. As a result, we have movies filled with
fantasy; we have amusement parks and novels that are
fantasy-laced. But the Bible warns us concerning the excess
of fantasy and fables. If we feed them continuously into our
mind and hearts, then our imaginations will reflect them.

The Word says:

*And they shall turn away their ears from the
truth, and shall be turned unto fables.*

2 Timothy 4:4

*For we have not followed cunningly devised
fables, when we made known unto you the power*

and coming of our Lord Jesus Christ, but were eyewitnesses of His majesty.

2 Peter 1:16

Neither give heed to fables and endless genealogies, which minister questions, rather than godly edifying which is in faith: so do.

I Timothy 1:4

An unhealthy exposure to fables, or fantasy, can cause you to lose your purpose. If you have been hurt, wounded or are under attack, the enemy will tempt you to **indulge** in fantasy as a way of escape. Before long, your godly imagination will be tainted by unreality.

Notice that the Word does not say that having fun is wrong. We can have fun, but we must also deal with reality. Instead the Word says that "turning away from the truth" towards fantasy, following fantasy, or giving heed to fantasy, is dangerous. It opens the door for the enemy to confuse you. The mind is impressive. Those who are hurting must be careful to not hang onto fantasy and embrace it as a way of life. Fantasy causes you to exalt yourself and you will lose your accuracy in the things of God. Remember, faith is not fantasy. Faith is a substance and a force that always produces.

Fantasy also causes your imagination to become passive. If your imagination is passive and empty, be sure that something will come to fill it. If our mind is filled with the whispers of the enemy, we will end up following them. Passivity of mind and imagination is an area of danger a believer can walk in.

If you overindulge in fantasy, you will become mentally depressed. People who live in a fantasy world do not face the real issues of life. One day they wake up and find their life has gone nowhere. They are so grieved and mentally depressed from it, that some commit suicide. These same people may have everything going for them. The problem was, they allowed their imagination to be manipulated by the devil through fantasy.

How to Recover

Protect the imagination that God has given you. Be aware of the schemes of the enemy. Keep your heart humble before the Lord.

Guide your imaginations into their proper channels by the Word of God. You are unlimited in what you can accomplish for the Kingdom of Heaven. God wants you to have a creative imagination. Do not let it go in the wrong direction. Line every imagination against the Word of God and ask yourself: **Is God exalted or I alone?**

If every believer would operate in the godly imagination offered to him, we would literally change the entire world for God.

Chapter 9

The Memory Under Attack

The human soul is a great entity. Every part of it expresses the character and personality of God. We have discussed the human will, the emotions, the intellect, the imagination. Although each area could have an entire book written on it alone; we have discussed them to the point of stability.

The last area of the soul is extremely important as well. The memory serves as our point of reference in every thought we have. Every scene we visually see, every thought we have, every word spoken to us, every thing we read, every thing we eat — any thing that crosses our path is automatically stored into our memory. The human memory is fascinating!

The memory is so valuable that when a person, through injury or disease, loses it, they no longer know who they are. They can no longer recognize sights that were once familiar to them. Although they can still have a will, an intellect, an imagination and emotions, they have lost their identity as a person.

Our memory has the power to conduct our way of life. For this very reason, your memory also must be ruled by your spirit or you cannot successfully fulfill the plan of God.

David's Power of Memory

Let's go again to the Book of I Samuel, chapter 17. The

life of David can show us the power of using our memory to fulfill the plan of God. We have already discussed how he used his imagination to slay Goliath. Now let's look at how he used his memory to bring him courage:

> *And Saul said to David, Thou art not able to go against this Philistine to fight with him: for thou art but a youth, and he a man of war from his youth.*
>
> *And David said unto Saul, Thy servant kept his father's sheep, and there came a lion, and a bear, and took a lamb out of the flock:*
>
> *And I went out after him, and smote him, and delivered it out of his mouth: and when he arose against me, I caught him by his beard, and smote him, and slew him.*
>
> *Thy servant slew both the lion and the bear: and this uncircumcised Philistine shall be as one of them, seeing he hath defied the armies of the living God.*
>
> *And David said moreover, The Lord that delivered me out of the paw of the lion, and out of the paw of the bear, he will deliver me out of the hand of this Philistine. And Saul said unto David, Go, and the Lord be with thee.*
>
> *Verses 33-37*

David relied on the power of his memory to give him the courage to believe God. He remembered how God had been with him in past trouble. Because of that great victory, he knew God would be with him in this feat as well. **His memory ignited his faith**; and he conquered the giant without fear.

That is the way our memory was created. **It was designed to bring into remembrance the good things in**

86

life and the Word of the Lord. It is to cause us to remember the faithfulness of God. Our memory can bring an unflinching trust in the plan of God.

Paul's Power of Memory

Paul said many similar things in the New Testament. One in particular is found in Second Timothy 4:17-18:

> *Notwithstanding the Lord stood with me, and strengthened me; that by me the preaching might be fully known, and that all the Gentiles might hear: and I was delivered out of the mouth of the lion.*
>
> *And the Lord shall deliver me from every evil work, and will preserve me unto his heavenly kingdom: to whom be glory forever and ever.*

Paul also relied on the power of his memory, to give him courage to fulfill his mission on the earth. He remembered that if God delivered him from evil before, He would do it again.

He also admonished Timothy to remember the prophecies that were spoken to him,

> *That thou by them mightest war a good warfare;*
>
> *Holding faith and having a good conscience; which some having put away concerning faith have made shipwreck.*
>
> *I Timothy 1:18-19*

In Second Timothy, chapter 1, we can read another exhortation to our memory:

> *Wherefore I put thee in remembrance that thou stir up the gift of God, which is in thee by the putting on of my hands,*

> *For God hath not given us the spirit of fear; but of power, and of love, and of a sound mind.*

> ### Verses 6-7

From these verses we can see if we stir up our memory for God, we will move in faith not fear. We will operate in power and godly love. Our godly memory causes us to retain a sound mind.

All through the Word of God we are exhorted to remember the stability from which we came, and to live by it.

If we can understand the positive attributes of a memory submitted to the Word of God, then we will see how the enemy attacks us.

Attack on the Memory

If the enemy can harass and torment your memory, he will paralyze you. It is that simple. I have seen men and women fall because of bad memories.

When we have been seriously hurt from an attack of the enemy, it sears our memory. If we do not deal with these memories and effectively recover from them, we will make the decisions of our lives based upon them. They bring a crippling and distracting effect upon our personality.

That is a terrible way to live. If we think about it, why should we base our lives on the hurts and wounds of the past? We must remember this important statement: **Your future is not based on the hurts of the past.** Everyone has been hurt and wounded at one time or another. **We cannot base the outcome of our future on past disappointments or past victories.** If we don't break free from that "claw", the enemy will direct our steps.

Amen

The devil uses our memory as an art gallery. He will cause similar painful circumstances to surround you, then say, "Remember how that hurt you? Let me walk you through the gallery of your hurts. See that? Remember this?" If we listen to it, we will succumb to fear and withdraw.

Fear causes withdrawal and paranoia. If the enemy has good access to our memory, every one we meet will be sized up according to our hurts. We are afraid to trust anyone. How can we walk in unity if we remain "an island to ourselves?" How can we thrust out into the confidence of God, if we mistrust all those called to help us? We cannot hide behind fear for very long. It is like a liquid chemical that boils inside of us, destroying the influence of God.

Fear

Fear is the force satan operates through, just as faith is the power that moves Heaven into the earth. Fear robs us of the faith of God. If faith produces life, health and peace; then fear produces death, disease and torment.

Fear robs us of a good conscience. Maybe you did something wrong. Maybe you gave into carnal sin. Even though you have repented and even though according to First John 1:9 you were absolutely forgiven, the enemy will attempt to rob you through your memory. When you go to pray for the sick, he will remind you of a sin, as though it was not forgiven. If you put that memory before the Word of the Lord, you will feel unworthy to be used by God. As a result, the sick will not receive the benefit of your prayer.

If the sin was against another person, a natural reconciliation is necessary also. Many times, that alone will shut the mouth of the enemy. But if you have done everything you know to do and harassment still persists, then begin to condemn what is condemning you. Reverse its effect and verbally condemn the torment with your mouth in Jesus' Name! If you allow the mental abuse to continue, your conscience will be marred.

mental abuse

When our good conscience is robbed by a memory, we lose effectiveness. We have a sense of unworthiness and inferiority. We feel insecure in everything we do, and it will show. That my friend, is a memory under attack.

Paul says a godly memory produces love. The opposite is true when the memory is under attack. A tormented mind produces hate and hardness. It operates in impulsiveness, trying to escape the torment of a bad memory. A tormented memory suspects evil in every person. It covers itself in a false pride. Because it operates from fear instead of faith, it has lost hope and cannot help others in trouble. If we nourish and feed a memory under attack, we will seek our own exaltation, rather than wait for the righteousness of God. A nurtured memory under attack has lost confidence and trust in God.

If we operate in this category for very long, we will lose the soundness of our mind. Mental wards are filled with hopeless victims, put there from nurtured hurts and wounds. When the soundness of our mind is gone, many complications set in. Medical science goes to great extremes to administrate peace to the patients. But in many, the sole source was a hurt left unresolved. Medication will not heal the hurt; it can only paralyze a memory.

We must fight for the power of our memory by the Word of God. **If God tells us repeatedly to "remember" His Word, then the plan of the enemy will cause you to forget it.**

How to Recover

Command the tormenting spirits to leave your memory. Purpose to forgive again those that have hurt you. Begin to look past the hurt into the faithfulness of God. He wants to work on your behalf.

If hurts have not entered in and sinful memories are

harassing you, then find scripture to fight back.

For example, in the Book of Job, chapter 31, verse 1, he fights an attack by this:

> *I made a covenant with mine eyes; why then should I think upon a maid?*

Job chose to covenant with his eyes, the mirror of his memory, that he would monitor what he looked upon. Purpose in your heart to do the same.

Maybe you have been paralyzed by fearful stories and events. Perhaps the enemy has reminded you that the same outcome will be in your life if you follow God. Fight back! Do not allow the devil to rob your destiny through fear. When David was afraid of his future due to stories of the past, he said:

> *Deliver me, O Lord, from mine enemies: I flee unto thee to hide me.*
>
> *Teach me to do thy will; for thou art my God: thy Spirit is good; lead me into the land of uprightness.*
>
> **Psalm 143:9-10**

Whatever situation you face, there is a sound cure for it in the Word of God. We must realize that the future is what I call "virgin territory". No man has yet walked into it. *The future is bright and does not have to be tainted by what we have already lived through.* Isaiah 43:18-19 speaks specifically of your future:

> *Remember ye not the former things, neither consider the things of old.*
>
> *Behold, I will do a new thing...*

The Apostle Paul says in Philippians 3:13-14:

...but this one thing I do, forgetting those things which are behind, and reaching forth unto those things which are before,

I press toward the mark for the prize of the high calling of God in Christ Jesus.

Paul recognized the power of his memory, good and bad. He made a statement in those verses, **that spoke loudly to his soul.** He emphasized that no matter what else he accomplished, his first priority was to,"forget the things that lay behind him" and press on into the future.

As leaders and believers, we must set our face like a flint and refuse to subject ourselves to the past. All of Heaven will work with you in your endeavor. Attitudes such as that attract the power of God. It draws strength and power to come into you. It produces invincible faith and will "move mountains."

You have the authority of your memory. You will choose the thoughts you meditate on. You were sent to the earth for a purpose. Do not lose it from a careless memory. **Gird up the loins of your mind, and conquer the ground placed before you!**

Chapter 10

The Human Body Under Attack

Just as the enemy can attack the soulish parts of a human being, that is not the end of his battleground. The human body is also a prime target, and it can be as greatly hindered as the soul of man.

The human body is our natural flesh, tissues, blood, membranes, organs and nervous system. The human body was given by God to show His handiwork; for us to live in and to carry the Gospel into the nations.

When we see acquaintances on the street, we recognize them by their human form. Or, when we hear their name, we visualize their human form in our minds. Each human body was created as an individual. Although some are identical twins, no one is created exactly alike.

The carnal man idolizes the human body. They do not look past the flesh and understand who the "real" man is. I have traveled all over the world, and without exception, there is a statue in every major city, idolizing a male or female physique. The natural man bases his entire selection of a mate on physique. The human body has the power to turn carnal men into fools.

Even though we recognize another person by human form, that is not the "real" person. That is their "shell," or what I call, their "body suit." The real person is the spirit man. The spirit man is eternal and lives forever. The body that so many idolize, will die.

Our body houses our spirit man. Our human body keeps our spirit man on the earth to fulfill the will of God. I like to express the difference between the two this way.

If we go to the moon, we must wear a space suit. Otherwise, because of lack of gravity, our bodies would leave the moon. The space suit holds our body to the surface of the moon.

The human body works in the same way for the spirit man. Your human body holds the spirit man to the earth. If your body dies, the spirit leaves. It cannot stay.

Your Body as a Vessel

Your human body is the vessel by which the Spirit speaks and moves. Your body is the vessel by which the Gospel is carried into the nations. Many times, God chooses to heal the afflictions of another *through* your human hands. He chooses to speak His oracles *through* your mouth. He desires to express His presence *through* your bodily presence in a room.

The human vessel has always been important in the plan of God. In the Book of Acts, Stephen understood this principle. He yielded his body to the Spirit of the Lord, and allowed his voice to be used to convict those around him. The religious leaders of the day had resisted the influence of the Holy Spirit up to that point. But the Word states in Acts 6:10, they could not resist His influence, *"when He spoke through a vessel."*

Jesus wants to live through your human body. He wants to come out and show His strength and compassion to the world. He desires for the scriptures to come alive through your mortal flesh.

He took the time while on earth, to not only show us the power in overcoming the soul, but He also paid for the

94

afflictions of our body. Not only did He take the sins of the world with Him to the Cross; He also took the diseases and sicknesses of the body. He shed His blood, paid for them, and pronounced healing for all who would believe Him.

If we do not take care of our physical bodies, our time on the earth can be cut short. Many great ministers of the past died early because they neglected their physical bodies. **Our bodies were not only created for our pleasure, but for the service of the Lord.**

In spite of all the medical terminology for the functions of the human body, if we can understand this one principle, then we can know the reasons for spiritual attacks against it.

Attack on the Human Body

The enemy attacks the human body in two categories: **by sense and by sickness.**

The human body houses five different senses: **sight, smell, sound, touch, and taste.** If these senses aren't modified, the devil will use them to tempt us into extremes.

The attack against our "senses" comes in the form of temptation. If we live a loose lifestyle and something looks tempting, smells nice, or feels good, then we can fall into sin. If we are unguarded, the sound of something can stimulate the human body to sin.

Television, billboards, magazines and other materials stimulate the senses of our human body. **If the enemy cannot attack you successfully in your soul, he will aim for your senses.** We must be careful what we gaze upon and what we listen to. When the flesh yields to these distractions, it cannot please God. Guard your senses, as they are the entrance to your human body.

Our human body is a seeker of its own pleasures. It

knows no limits. It will go after anything, and doesn't know when to stop on its own. Every craving the body has, must be controlled.

The second way the enemy attacks the body is through sickness and disease. The devil wants to hinder your labor for the Lord and even destroy your flesh to get you off the planet. He does not want the power of God revealed through your vessel. If he cannot destroy your soul, he will attempt to devastate your flesh.

Jesus hates sickness and disease because it destroys our bodies. He is not intimidated by it, nor does it influence His power. He hates it because it hurts humanity. Part of the Great Commission in preaching the Gospel is to heal the sick and all manner of disease. A large portion of Jesus' ministry was healing the sick. He heals because of His love and compassion towards us. He does not want the human body to suffer.

When we have been under attack mentally for a period of time, it will begin to spread in our human body. Sometimes, the enemy will put symptoms on you that seem real, but cannot be medically explained. This is nothing but an attack on your physical body.

How to Recover

Do not give in to the manifestations of these attacks! Stand against them, and call them for what they are. Be led by the Spirit, do something contrary to these symptoms. Call upon the resurrection strength of the Lord to come into you. Command pain to go and refuse the entrance of it. Many times, **fear** is the spirit that keeps these symptoms working in you. I have talked with many people plagued by migraine headaches. One in particular said that each time one came, they checked themselves to see if they feared something. When the area was discovered, they rebuked the fear, and the pain left immediately.

Don't let the devil torment your time of rest and sleep. Calm your thoughts and speak peace to them.

Quote the Word of God:

I will both lay me down in peace and sleep: for thou, Lord, only makest me dwell in safety.

Psalms 4:8

If the enemy can rob your rest, he will gain entrance into your soul. Many people have fallen into sin due to lack of rest. You must take care of the physical man through eating habits, exercise and rest. You cannot work all the time and keep your mind buzzing when you should be sleeping. If you are physically tired, it is hard to gain spiritual strength. In the Book of Daniel, part of the job of the enemy is to, "wear out the saints" (7:25). **It is the will of God that you rest, sleep and renew yourself.**

If you need a physical healing from actual disease in your body, then keep believing the Word of God. Listen to anointed preaching of the Word that professes and believes in the healing power of God. Read testimonies of healings. Build up your faith to receive God's best.

God desires that we give our bodies to Him as a living sacrifice (Romans 12:1). This isn't a dead, lifeless sacrifice; but a living, healthy one. He desires the willful control of our bodies and our senses. He wants to live through them and show the world His love and power.

In Philippians 1:20, Paul had this to say:

According to my earnest expectation and my hope, that in nothing I shall be ashamed, but that with all boldness, as always, so now also Christ shall be magnified in my body, whether it be by life, or by death.

Becoming "dead" to your flesh does not mean that life will cease to be exciting. Allowing Christ to live through your human body is the most thrilling experience on earth. Do not allow the enemy to cheat you from knowing His life through you.

Chapter 11

The Human Spirit Under Attack

Our spirit man is the direct channel between God and ourselves. We receive instruction, direction and purpose from our spirit man. We follow the unctions of the Holy Spirit in our spirit and direct the rest of our lives from the warnings we sense from it.

The spirit man is the primary seat of our entire being. We were created spirit first; then body and soul.

Although our spirit man follows the same commandments that every other believer follows, it is still an individual. Each spirit man has a different call and a different function to make the Body of Christ complete. Your spirit man will express itself to the degree you submit to God. Your spirit man is unlimited in potential and purpose. It feeds and nurtures itself from the Word of God.

Proverbs 20:27 says:

The spirit of man is the candle of the Lord...

Your spirit man is the light of God to the world. That is why the spirit must affect our soul and our body. The Bible did not say our emotions or our flesh was the light of the world. The Bible says Jesus, from our spirit man, is the Light to the world. Our soul and body only reflect the light of our spirit and express it.

Although being filled with Jesus helps us become the candle to the world, it is still our choice whether or not to "let it shine." The Bible clearly states that if we, *"live by the spirit"* we must learn to also, *"walk by the spirit"* (Galatians 5:25).

As a believer, once we are born again, we must learn the operations of our spirit according to the Word of God. We must learn the character of God Himself, and the movements of our spirit toward Him. We must learn how to abide by the spirit and to not quench its actions. We must learn to base our decisions upon the unction within us and follow it. As we discipline ourselves to the workings of our spirit, then we will become "strong in spirit" and are useful to the purpose of God.

It is in this area the enemy attempts his attack.

Attack on the Spirit Man

As we have already discussed, the enemy tries first for the soul and body of man. His purpose is to shut off the outlet we have of expressing Jesus to the world.

But when a man is spiritual, and the body and soul are totally subject to his spirit, then the attack will hit the spirit man immediately.

If the man is ignorant of the devices of the enemy, he will succumb to his tactics.

Is it possible for a man to have his body and soul subjected to the Word of God and still be ignorant of the attack on his spirit? Yes!

Even while disciplining your flesh and soul, if you have lost your joy, your liberty of expression and your spiritual perceptions, then your spirit is under attack.

Some of the most sincere believers, adamantly trying to renew their minds in the area of body and soul, have lost their sense of righteousness. They have feelings of total unworthiness and base the discipline of their body and soul on this basis.

What was once an exciting spiritual frontier, has now become a "box" and they have lost their vision.

We must understand, the main function of the spirit man is revelation. The spirit man is the highest creative power inside of us. Revelation should abound in every form of our walk with God. **Revelation should come to us in every area; from the lost on the street corner, to the depths of the Word.**

Loss of Accuracy

In true guidance from the Spirit of God, your human spirit and a renewed, mature mind work together. Your spirit gets the plan and unction; and your mind agrees with the Word of God in the situation. The guidance is not impulsive, and your intelligence is not in constant rebellion to it.

We must be careful when we think our mind will be in *constant* disagreement with the Holy Spirit. When we think this way, our common sense leaves us. It is true that the law of God is spiritual; but that is the reason we are constantly *renewing* our minds to His Word. When we receive instruction from the Holy Spirit, if our mind has been renewed in the Word, it will *submit* to the Word and the plan. Even if the mind does not understand, if it has been renewed, it will agree in *faith* with the plan before you.

There will be certain situations that call for a quick and seemingly impulsive response or action. These situations usually mean life or death; and the mind doesn't have the time to think. You move in these situations from the prompting of the Holy Spirit through you. But in the long-range plan of God, the renewed mind must be in a "faith agreement" with the Holy Spirit. When we shut our minds off, we open ourselves to a driving spirit.

When a person is "driven," he is out of cooperation with God. A driven person is a never-ending cycle. Being in their presence is exhausting. Even their words weary you. They begin to look old and tired far ahead of their years. (The quickening Spirit of the Lord causes youthfulness to come and brings life to your flesh.)

Being spiritually driven is extremely dangerous. If someone is driven, they are under attack. If they are under attack, portions of their life will not "add up" according to the Word of God. This is where dangerous deception enters in. Just because they had success in one area, they expect others to assume *every area* of their life is also led by God. When a person is driven, they are exceptionally hardened to human needs and desires. As a result, they become a "taskmaster" and insinuate everyone is to follow that direction or they are not following God. This attack of the enemy is not only centered to destroy the driven vessel, but countless others as well.

Spiritual Wisdom

We need to understand that since we are spiritual, we are open to the entire spiritual realm — good and evil. Just because something comes to you spiritually, does not mean it is from God. You must line up every thought and unction according to the character and Word of God. If we think every thought and unction comes from the Spirit of God, then we are setting ourselves up to be infallible and are sure to be misled.

How can you know if your spirit man is under attack? **If the plan or purpose you feel pulls you out from a deeper fellowship with God, it is from the enemy.** It doesn't matter how good it seems. It doesn't matter how much it promises, or how much potential is there for a "great work." If your fellowship with God decreases from it, it was not from Him. To fulfill a true unction from God, we must rely on a constant relationship with Him to complete it.

If your spirit is depressed, has lost joy and peace, creativity and liberty, it is under attack. When you feel an overwhelming unction to act emotional and frenzied, your spirit is under attack. When you are driven beyond normal means, and your fellowship with God is side-tracked from a "spiritual" desire, you are under attack.

If you are in this area of attack, then get "back to basics." **Refuse** to be driven. **Refuse** to let your fellowship with God be side-tracked. **Refuse** impulsive desires to take action. Learn to season yourself by the Word and under the authority of good leadership.

The greatest need of the church is to know and understand the laws of the Spirit. Fully maturing our spirit man produces accuracy in our co-workings with God. The loss of spiritual accuracy has hurt every move of God in the earth. When we get caught up in the movings of God, and refuse to take the time in maturing our own spirit man, revival will be short-lived. Strong and stable accuracy must come forth.

Take the time to invest in your spirit man. Not only will it cause you to fulfill the destiny on your life, but the end results will bring maturity into every life you meet.

Chapter 12

The Recovery Zone

The purpose of this book is to alert us in the different areas of attack. In the past, we have been too vague in the area of spiritual battles. Most believers know they are under attack, but cannot describe it.

It is important that we learn to accurately discern where we are being attacked and why. If we can understand the area, we will know how to effectively recover.

In the conclusion, there are just a few points I want to leave with you.

When you have been in a spiritual war, you've stood and you've won, **you still need time to recover.** Know that.

Sometimes we say "hallelujah! It's over!" and think we can run the race at the same pace as before. We think everything is over and we can go right on as before.

Many who have successfully won during the attack fall backwards during recovery.

Why? They don't understand that **it takes time** to build strength again. They think because they aren't quite as sharp as before, they are still in a war. They fight something that isn't there. Finally, they're worn out and discouraged. They just give up.

Just as your body needs to recover from a physical illness, it must also recover from a spiritual attack. Think for a minute. After the initial sickness is gone from you, and you feel better, you can't run a marathon yet! The sickness is gone, the battle is over, but your body needs time to regain strength. **The same is true in the spiritual realm.**

Don't rush yourself. Let God have time to work for you. Give yourself room to grow and mature in the things you have been through.

Remember not to overestimate or underestimate the war you have gone through. It is commendable that you made it; give God the credit and use the wisdom it has produced in you. God likes to encourage you; so let Him.

Encouragement aides in your recovery and healing. Allow yourself to be the son or daughter of God, and let Him be the Father to you. It's good to hear Him talk to you and point out what the two of you did together. Let Him do it and rejoice with Him.

Remember these other basic points of recovery:

1. Pray in tongues.

The Amplified Version of Jude 20 says it best:

> *But you, beloved, build yourselves up (founded) on your most holy faith (make progress, rise like an edifice higher and higher), praying in the Holy Spirit.*

I like that translation because it paints a picture of what faith mixed with praying in tongues can accomplish. An "edifice" is a structure. Websters Dictionary defines it as "a large or splendid building." **Your faith, kindled by the Word and praying in tongues, causes you to rise and solidify yourself into a mighty, towering force.** No wind of doctrine or controversy can shake you when the two are combined within you. When we build ourselves up by prayer and the Word, our house will stand when trouble comes. Our fervent prayer avails much (James 5:16).

2. Sit under a good anointing. Feed on the Word — the Bread of Life.

When you are recovering, the Word of God that is delivered under a good anointing is like cool streams of water to your whole man. Understanding and revelation comes when the preaching is clear and sharp. You'll hear God in new dimensions when you sit yourself under a leader that hears from Heaven. Read and devour the Word of God. It will strengthen and feed you, making you strong and unconquerable.

3. Worship God in the privacy of your devotion time.

This is not the time to be silent. Lift your hands, open your mouth and praise the Lord! Dance before Him, and receive the joy of His strength into your being. When you worship in spirit and truth, it enables you to walk above circumstances and controversy. Then join yourself with the congregation of the saints, and pierce the heavenlies with strength and praise.

4. Confession of the Word.

Find the scriptures that speak directly to your heart in this time of your life. These scriptures mean life for you. Speak them out of your heart and allow them to transform your thinking and circumstances. The Word of God was designed to fight and take pressure from you. It promises to complete the mission it was sent to do, it will never return void or incomplete, and it will prosper in the areas spoken to (Isaiah 55:11).

5. Have someone pray for you. Their prayers can add to your recovery.

Your most trusted, spiritual friend knows how to pray for you. The Bible says that one can put a thousand to flight, two can put ten thousand away (Deut. 32:30). Why do alone what two together can accomplish?

6. Listen to good Gospel tapes; read good Gospel books.

We don't always have the time to sit, read and pray. Thank God for tape players! Put in a good Gospel tape and allow it to minister to you as you go about your daily work. Instead of reading the newspaper or a popular magazine, read the story of a great man or woman of God. Read about their trials and temptations and how they overcame them to complete the plan of God. Read books on faith, healing or deliverance. Allow good Gospel books to supplement the Word of God in your life and add to your understanding and application.

7. Fellowship with good Christian people.

This subject is so in-depth, I could write another book on it alone! Find the people that uplift and encourage you. Surround yourself with those that know how to laugh and bring godly joy into your life. Fellowship with those that have the same morals, the same fervency for God and the same purpose. Friends that fear the Lord bring a good balance into your life. Through the right associations and connections, your life can be enhanced and *"sharpened like iron"* (Proverbs 27:17). If you don't have any godly friends, ask God to bring them into your life. He will never fail you.

Now, let me pray for you:

"Father, thank You for opening the eyes of our understanding. We believe there is no attack planned against us that we cannot win. We ask You to show us the areas that will bring total victory. Show us Your plan and we will follow.

Right now, I pray for the healing of mental disorders to come to the people. I command the spirits of harassment and torment to leave, in Jesus' Name. I speak by the power of God, a soundness of mind into their being.

I speak peace into the nervous system; for Your

108

righteousness to come forth in every area of their soul.

I reverse the curse against the people of God, and condemn the spirits condemning them. I say that every false, driving way cannot manifest in their lives and ministries. I pray for accuracy to come into the lives of Your people. The plans and purposes of Heaven must come into the earth!

I believe for the past hurts and wounds to cease in their effects. I come against every adverse manifestation that is contrary to the Word of God.

Father, I believe for strength to come into the hearts of the people; for forgiveness and wisdom to come in their relationships. Enhance the godly associations in their lives. Bring to them the friends that reverence Your Name.

Thank You Father, that when we pray, You hear from Heaven and answer. Cause Yourself to become real to Your people, and show Yourself in their lives.

I stand and believe for them, in Jesus' Name."

To contact Roberts Liardon
write:

Roberts Liardon Ministries
P.O. Box 30710
Laguna Hills, CA 92654

Please include your prayer requests and comments when you write.

Additional copies of this book are available
from your local bookstore or by contacting:

Embassy Publishing
P.O. Box 3500
Laguna Hills, CA 92654

Other Books by Roberts Liardon

Run to the Battle
Learning To Say No Without Feeling Guilty
I Saw Heaven
Success in Life and Ministry
The Invading Force
The Quest for Spiritual Hunger
The Price of Spiritual Power
Breaking Controlling Powers
Religious Politics
Cry of the Spirit
Spiritual Timing

New From Harrison House

Kathryn Kuhlman

Videos by Roberts Liardon

The Lord Is a Warrior
I Saw Heaven
The Roar of the '90s
Developing An Excellent Spirit
No More Walls
Confronting the Brazen Heavens
Reformers and Revivalists
God's Generals

Available from your local
bookstore or by writing:

Roberts Liardon Ministries
P. O. Box 30710, Laguna Hills, CA 92654